CONQUEST OR LOSS . . .

No doubt, the U.S. airmen at Biak, Noemfoor, Sansapor, and Morotai felt an envy for the combat crews in the Philippines. Those airmen up north were in the real war, making strikes on plump shipping, hitting fat targets in the ground war, and brawling with Japanese air units in regular dogfights, where the enemy usually lost by a lopsided score.

However, conditions would change abruptly for Maj. Glen Doolittle of the 345th Group, Maj. Bill Dunham of the 460th Squadron, Maj. Bill Cowper of the 70th Squadron, and Maj. Ed Gavin of the 38th Bomb Group. Within the next two or three days they would become part of the biggest aircraft strikes against ships since the Battle of the Bismarck Sea. Further, the stakes in this battle would be extremely high for U.S. forces—the conquest or the loss of Leyte.

MORE FANTASTIC READING!

VALOR AT LEYTE

BY LAWRENCE CORTESI

ZEBRA BOOKS
KENSINGTON PUBLISHING CORP.

ZEBRA BOOKS

are published by

KENSINGTON PUBLISHING CORP.
475 Park Avenue South
New York, N.Y. 10016

Printed in the United States of America

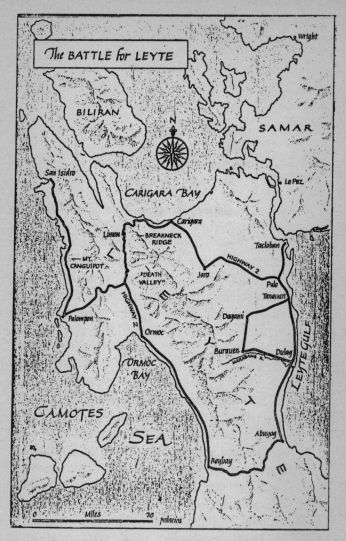

U.S. forces had advanced in Leyte to Breakneck Ridge, Burauen, and beyond Abuyog before being stopped by stubborn Japanese resistance.

VALOR AT LEYTE

Chapter One

The United States, in one of its biggest military operations of World War II, invaded Leyte in the Philippine Islands on 20 October 1944. If the Americans occupied the island and established strong air and naval bases, they would cut off the Japanese lifeline between her homelands and the East Indies, where Japan got the bulk of her raw materials to carry on the war. Thus, the Japanese spared no effort to stop the Americans at Leyte.

"The war would be won or lost at Leyte," said Field Marshal Count Hisaichi Terauchi, the CinC of the Southern Region Forces that included all army, navy, and air units in the western Pacific. "Thus, we initiated the TA Operation to send enough reinforcements into Leyte to contain the American invaders, and perhaps drive them off this island altogether. Such a defeat would have been disastrous for the United States in her war with Japan."

The Japanese showed great determination in this operation for within a week of the Leyte invasion, they had poured an entire new division and tons of supplies into the island to stop the American drive inland. Gen. Walter Krueger, Cinc of the U.S. 6th Army, soon realized that the conquest of Leyte might be one of the most exhaustive operations of the war.

"We were shocked by the tenacious Japanese defense in Leyte," Krueger said. "After the landings, we quickly captured the Tacloban and Dulag airfields. But, as our ground forces moved inland, the Japanese slowed us to a halt, while they poured reinforcements into the island. If they could hold us long enough, they might turn the Leyte fight into another gruelling Guadalcanal campaign."

On 30 October 1944, Col. Tom Clifford of the U.S. 24th Infantry Division's 34th Regiment was struggling over rough, rain-soaked terrain from his beachhead at Tacloban. Clifford's GIs had been plodding along Highway 2, northwest and meeting stubborn resistance along the way by fanatic Japanese troops of the 68th Brigade that had been fighting since the American invasion on 20 October. The Nippon soldiers, half starved, ill clothed, and poorly armed, nonetheless showed a persistence that the Americans had not seen since the early New Guinea campaign. The seaport town of Carigara, on Carigara Bay on Leyte's north coast, lay only 22 miles from Tacloban. Yet, the U.S. 34th Infantry Regiment had not captured the town until 25 October, five days after the invasion. Rugged mountains, stifling humidity, insect plagued jungles, and drenching rains had helped the Japanese to stall the American advance. Further, the newly arrived 46th Regiment of the Japanese 1st Division had joined the 68th Brigade.

Only a few miles west of Carigara, the GIs ran into the Limon Hills where Highway 2 snaked through dense, uphill terrain before coming down into the town of Limon in Canguiput Province in western Leyte. However, the 24th U.S. Infantry troops now ran into even more stubborn defenses by the Japanese 46th Regiment and 68th Brigade. The defenders defiantly held their ground.

Maj. Ed Edris, the executive officer of the 34th Regiment, brought Colonel Clifford more discouraging news. "We can't budge them, sir. They're dug in like moles, with mortar units, machine gun teams, rifle squads, and even artillery."

"Goddamn," Clifford scowled, "we've been hitting the bastards with air attacks and artillery for the past three days."

The major shook his head. "No matter how hard we hit, they don't cave in, and I think they've brought in an entire new regiment of troops."

"This Leyte campaign seems hopeless," Clifford said.

"Every time we launch a new attack, they drive us back," Edris said. "I must tell you, Colonel, we've suffered considerable casualties. I don't think we're going to clear the Nips off those ridges until we bring in real heavy artillery and plenty of tanks."

The GIs of the 34th Regiment had named this

hill between Carigara and Limon the Breakneck Ridge, for the American dogfaces had endured severe casualties and deep frustration in their attempts to wrest the ridges from the Japanese. And more agonizing were the heavy rains that continually left the dogfaces soaked and uncomfortable in their mud-caked bivouac tents, where each day they ate unappetizing K rations or an occasional hot C ration meal that was only slightly more palatable. Further, humidity and insects plagued the GIs constantly, while in the evening, they enjoyed little sleep because the Washboard Charlies of the Japanese 4th Base Air Force came over every night to drop confettis of 21 pound bomb clusters indiscriminately on their positions.

Col. Tom Clifford scowled when he got this latest report from his executive officer. He could not believe their slow progress. In the sea battles around Leyte, the U.S. 5th Fleet had almost destroyed the Japanese navy in the enemy's ill fated Sho Plan to destroy the Leyte beachheads. By this 30th of October, the enemy had few warships left. Also, U.S. carrier planes had flattened one Japanese airbase after another in the northern Philippines, while the army's U.S. 5th Air Force had leveled most of the Japanese airfields in the southern Philippines. Yet the enemy's air force seemed to have an inexhaustible supply of planes and plenty of untouched airfields, since they could bomb U.S. positions in Leyte with damaging regularity.

"I'll order more air strikes," Major Edris said, interrupting Colonel Clifford's meditations.

The 34th Regiment commander nodded.

But despite their much more superior resources, the Americans continued to suffer serious difficulties during the first ten days on Leyte. Adm. Thomas Kinkaid of the U.S. 5th Fleet had complained bitterly because the army had not completed work on the Tacloban and Dulag airfields to bring in land based bombers. The navy's warships and carriers needed to resupply and refuel, but General MacArthur had insisted that the carriers and warships remain in the area because of "unforeseen circumstances." Drenching rains and Japanese air attacks had delayed the completion of the airstrips for housing Army Air Force bombers. The heavy downpours had washed away the leveled runways faster than engineers could repair them, and the Japanese air units had punched holes in the runways regularly with their 550 pound bombs. Thus, only three squadrons of P-38 fighter planes were thus far based in Leyte, and General Whitehead of the 5th Air Force could not even guess when he could bring in the bulk of his aircraft.

Atop Breakneck Ridge, the terrain under the dense jungle trees looked like a punchboard. Dozens of spider shaped trenches dotted the area. The Japanese defenders had firmly established themselves in a maze of holes with interlocking tunnels, so the defenses of the 46th Regiment and 68th Brigade could easily shelter its troops safely when P-38 fighter-bombers unleashed strafing fire or GP bombs on the ridges. Invariably, after an air attack or an artillery barrage, the Japanese

11

hurried back to their defense posts in time to meet any new American infantry assault on Breakneck Ridge.

The Japanese defenders, including 600 men of the 68th Brigade's 1st Battalion, had shown phenomenal grit in holding out against superior numbers of better trained and better equipped troops. From their high ground entrenchments, they fought tenaciously, spurred by the news that new supplies and more troops would join them as did the 46th Regiment.

On this same 30 October day that Major Edris and Colonel Clifford bemoaned their inability to take the ridge, Maj. Aesada Shigehara, CO of the 1st Battalion, met with Capt. Hokio Saito, his executive officer.

"Our brave troops have effectively repulsed the latest Yankee assault," Shigehara said, "but we may expect another American attack."

"The men are exhausted, Major," Saito answered. "They are weak and they are having difficulty in subsisting on one rice ball a day. Even with these fresh troops of the 1st Division we are hard pressed. It is only the expectation that perhaps more food and supplies will arrive that keeps our soldiers fighting."

Shigehara grinned and picked up a sheet from his makeshift desk in the tent under the jungle trees. "I have good news, Captain. More reinforcements will be here soon. But more than that," he gestured. "These new troops will not merely join us, but will relieve us and the 68th Brigade will return to Manila for rest."

Saito's eyes widened.

"I have been informed that the other two regiments of the 1st Division will arrive in Leyte to join their other regiment and relieve our own battle weary brigade."

"Our prayers are answered," Saito grinned.

"You will inform our soldiers at once," Shigehara said. "Implore them to hold their positions no matter how harshly the enemy attacks again. They must hold, for the rewards will be worthwhile."

"I will do so," Captain Saito promised.

The troops of Shigehara's battalion, informed of their impending relief, reacted positively. They would continue to hold Breakneck Ridge while they awaited the other 1st Division regiments. The 1st, also known as the Gem Division, because of their impressive record in the China fighting, had been established in 1874, and had seen action on the Asian continent for decades.

This crack division had won great victories during the Sino-Japanese and Russo-Japanese wars before a recall to Tokyo. The division had next left their homeland during the 1930's to win impressive battles against the Chinese. Every soldier in the Japanese army considered an assignment to the Gem Division as the fulfillment of his military ambition. Now, at the request of General Yamashita, who directed operations in the Philippines, Imperial Headquarters had agreed to send this unit into the Philippines to stop the Americans at Leyte.

Some 30 miles southwest of the ridge, the GIs of

the 7th Division had moved west from Dulag, but the Japanese had stopped them cold at Burauen. 7,000 troops of the Japanese 102nd and 16th Divisions were entrenched in hill positions. The Americans' lead 1st Battalion of the 32nd Regiment had come about six miles west of Dulag when they met fierce resistance from Japanese defenders, the 13th Regiment under Col. Jiro Saito. Continually, Japanese 37mm and 75mm guns boomed from the Burauen hills into the advancing Americans and the U.S. 32nd Regiment GIs remained dug in. At dark on this 30 October, the regimental commander, Col. John Finn, met with his 2nd Battalion CO, Lt. Col. James Pearsall.

"Have recon patrols brought back any information yet?" Finn asked.

"Some," Pearsall nodded.

"Well?"

"It's bad, real bad," the 2nd Battalion commander answered. "Patrols tell us the Nips are dug in along a five mile stretch of hills. They've got artillery in there, all kinds of machine gun positions, and God only knows how many mortars."

"We've got to get through," Finn grumbled. "We've got to reach the west coast and close in on Ormoc. 6th Army headquarters says the Japanese are pouring all kinds of reinforcements onto the island through Ormoc Bay. It's obvious the Nips won't spare anything to hold their positions on Leyte."

"Our guys are moving slowly everywhere,

14

Colonel," Pearsall said. "Up north they stopped the 24th cold west of Carigara. The 96th in the south is stalled west of Abuyog, and we're pretty much bogged down here in the center. We need more support, sir; more air and artillery fire, and maybe even tanks if they can get some armor up here from Dulag."

Colonel Finn nodded and he then gestured. "I want your battalion to make another attack at first light along the river route. I'll send out patrols tonight to find a weak spot. They must have one somewhere."

"Yes sir."

The next morning, 31 October, Maj. James Pearsall led a 600 man force into the Burauen Hills, skirting the Marabang River with his GIs and hoping to scale the ridge on the flank to overrun the defenders. Pearsall led his troops along the stream for two miles and then sent out a patrol to probe Japanese defenses. The squad returned an hour later to report some entrenched machine gunners along the edge of the winding road. Pearsall called for air attacks and a squadron of P-38 fighter-bombers from the 49th Fighter Group came out of Leyte's Tacloban airstrip to rake the Japanese positions with strafing fire and bombs. But like the other dug-in Japanese, these at Burauen had also burrowed deep into interlacing positions to shelter themselves from air attacks. By the time the Lightnings had droned away, the Japanese defenders had returned to their positions.

At 1015 hours, amidst a driving rain, Pearsall

led his troops up the slope through thick jungles. But Japanese spotters in the trees saw the GIs and they alerted defenders. The American dogfaces had hoped to use the heavy rain squalls and dense brush to obscure themselves so they could surprise the Japanese. However, as the GIs came within 25 or 30 yards of the defense positions, chattering machine gun fire and thumping mortar shells greeted the Americans. More than a dozen U.S. infantrymen fell dead and another ten suffered wounds. Pearsall quickly retreated down the heavily forested slopes.

Again, the Americans had failed to make a dent in the enemy's 13th Regiment positions.

In the early afternoon, Colonel Finn angrily called 7th Division headquarters in Dulag. "Goddamn it," he screamed at the operations chief, "where are those tanks you promised us? We got hurt again this morning trying to break through those Nip defenses. We need tanks!"

"I'm sorry, Colonel, the roads are impassable with these heavy rains and Japanese air raids. Armor just bogs down. I can only tell you that we'll have those Shermans out there as soon as possible. Just keep the pressure on those enemy positions. You'll get more air strikes this afternoon."

"Sure," Finn grumbled, "and those bastard Washboard Charlies will bomb us again tonight. I thought we knocked out the Jap air force."

"Just hang on, Colonel."

Thus the 32nd Regiment, like other units of the U.S. 6th Army, remained stalled in their westward drive. Colonel Finn was frustrated because he too believed that the longer the ground war stood at a standstill, the more time the Japanese had to bring in reinforcements for strengthening their defenses.

In fact, inside a tent headquarters in the mountainous jungle terrain of the Burauen hills, Col. Jiro Saito of the 16th Division's 13th Regiment met with his battalion commanders, Maj. Maeda Kamijo and Maj. Suzu Tatrishi.

"I offer you my thanks for the excellent defense by you and your soldiers," the colonel began. "The enemy has failed to dislodge us from our positions here in the Burauen sector. Despite their naval strength, the enemy has not stopped the flow of reinforcements in men and supplies to Leyte, while the brave airmen of our air force continues to harass the enemy daily."

"We will not fail, Honorable Saito," Major Kamijo said.

The 13th Regiment commander nodded, but he then squeezed his face. "We can thank our heavenly ancestors that our troops have performed so admirably while they subsist under these horrible conditions. I grieve because these courageous men have not had enough food and they live under the most rudimentary circumstances."

"It is the hope of more reinforcements that sustains them, Colonel," Major Tatrishi said.

"Perhaps this hope will be fulfilled," the 13th Regiment commander said. He picked up a sheet from his log hewn desk and waved the paper before his commanders. "This report is from 35th Army headquarters. The renowned 26th Division

17

along with many tons of food and supplies are expected to arrive soon in Leyte. Troops of the 26th Division will join us at Burauen to mitigate the hardship of our own troops and to feed their bellies.''

"Perhaps our regiment will be relieved," Major Kamijo grinned.

"Our soldiers deserve such relief," Saito said, "for we have been fighting viciously and with no rest since the American invasion." He gestured and spoke again. "Return to your units. Tell your soldiers that they are a credit to the Imperial forces in showing so much courage and determination. You may also tell your troops that supplies are on the way to ease their burdens."

At Abuyog to the south, Col. Edwin May, CO of the 96th Division's 383rd Regiment, sat in a thatched hut that served as his headquarters. Capt. Hugh Young of the regiment's C Company sat across from him. Young wore a distressed look on his face.

"I'm sorry, sir, we just can't make a dent in those Japanese defenses. They're dug in too strongly on the Visayan Mountain Range. Unless we get more air strikes, a lot more artillery, and a cut-off of their supplies, we'll never move them out of those hills."

Colonel May scowled. "Son of a bitch; this Leyte campaign is turning into the worst mess we've had in the Pacific so far."

The captain shook his head. "The Nips keep getting reinforcements and more supplies into Baybay, south of Ormoc. How come the air force can't stop them?"

"They don't have enough planes in Tacloban and no bombers at all," May said. "5th Air Force says they'll have bombers in Leyte as soon as they can get the air fields ready for them."

"Yes sir," Captain Young answered.

But, there was little confidence or enthusiasm in the C Company commander's voice. He had been stalled here at the foot of the Visayan Mountains for several days, fighting for every yard of terrain. Air strikes by both army and navy air units had done little to break the Japanese defenses. But, like other 35th Army units, the Nippon troops in the southern sector had built a web of interlocking dugouts that defied both artillery barrages and air strikes. Unless they lost the continuing flow of supplies, the Japanese could hold out indefinitely.

Atop a forested ridge west of Abuyog, Gen. Shimpei Fukue, commander of the Japanese 102nd Division and the southern sector itself, peered through field glasses at the American entrenchments in the distance. He had occasionally unleashed artillery barrages which had forced the Americans to run for cover. Fukue was apparently content to maintain the stalemate, hoping to wear out the Americans, until the arrival of combat units of the 30th Division from Mindanao which were expected to get here soon. Next to Fukue stood Col. Nosua Kokuda, commander of the 102nd Division's 20th Regiment.

"They are frustrated, General, utterly at a loss."

"We will do more than stop them when our

reinforcements arrive," Fukue said. "I was told by the Honorable Suzuki that massive numbers of troops and many tons of supplies are coming to Leyte. If we hold the enemy for the time being, we can surely conduct a counteroffensive when such reinforcements arrive."

"Yes, Honorable Fukue," Colonel Kakuda said.

"We will check our defense," the general gestured, "to make certain all troops are on full alert. The Americans may attempt to make still more useless attacks."

"Yes, General," Kakuda said again.

Thus did the stalemate on Leyte continue over the next two days. Units of the U.S. 24th Division could not dislodge the 38th Brigade and 46th Regiment troops in the north. 7th Division units could not dislodge the Japanese defenders in the center at Burauen, and 7th Division troops could not dislodge General Fukue's forces beyond Abuyog in the south.

Eleven days after the Leyte invasion, the Americans were mired in a bitter ground war that could well get much worse. Philippine guerillas had joined the Americans in the many areas of Leyte, reconnoitering enemy positions, engaging in sabotage, and even fighting alongside the GIs. Still, the Japanese held on stubbornly and even saw a chance to win the battle for Leyte.

The Americans knew that the Japanese had discharged the equivalent of a full fresh division on the west coast of Leyte during the past week. They had also landed many smaller units which

20

had come from across the Camotes Sea from Cebu. As the Japanese continued to send reinforcements into Leyte through Ormoc Bay, the U.S. 5th Air force continually sent out planes from Tacloban to attack shipping in the shipping lanes between Manila and Ormoc Bay. The Americans had also sent heavy bombers from New Guinea to hit shipping and to attack airfields, while U.S. Navy carrier groups also made air attacks on shipping and airdromes.

American airmen had sunk two cruisers, some destroyers, and several marus since the invasion of Leyte. U.S. flyers had also destroyed supply dumps. However, the Americans had not stemmed the flow of troops and supplies into Leyte. Japanese merchant ships always had destroyer escorts, whose gunners were quite adept with anti-aircraft fire. And quite often, swarms of Zeros or Oscars hung over the reinforcement flotillas to intercept U.S. planes which had attempted to attack the convoys.

Almost invariably, when Japanese fighter pilots engaged in combat with American P-38 pilots out of Tacloban, the Japanese got mauled. Between 26 October and 2 November, in a half dozen dogfights over the Sibuyan and Camotes Seas, the U.S. army and naval airmen downed 121 Japanese planes to a loss of 16 of their own.

Still, the Japanese losses in aircraft was a small price for the successful disembarkment of reinforcements and supplies in Leyte. The success of this current version of the old Tokyo Express runs had enabled the Japanese to hold their own in the

Leyte ground fighting as they had done two years earlier at Guadalcanal.

Yet for the Japanese, the fighting in the Philippines carried with it an ominous possibility: as the Guadalcanal campaign had offered the Americans the first opportunity to crack the Japanese Pacific empire, the Leyte campaign now offered the Americans an opportunity to deal a lethal blow to this same Japanese Pacific empire.

The two adversaries recognized the high stakes involved in Leyte, and both sides were determined to win. The Japanese planned to accelerate their reinforcements into Leyte with more troops and supplies so they could drive their enemy back into the sea. The Americans were equally determined to build up forces on Leyte so they could crush the island's defenders.

The Japanese and the Americans thus prepared for another classic confrontation in the Pacific war. But, ironically, while the two sides planned a strategy that would assure victory in a great land battle amid the rugged jungles and mountains of Leyte, the victory would be decided not on land, but on the sea and in the air.

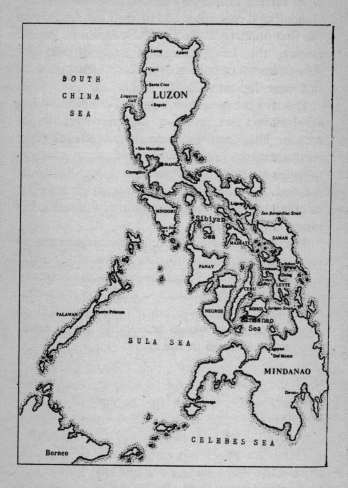

The Philippine Islands—Japanese had been running reinforcement convoys from Manila down through Sibuyan Sea to Leyte's Ormoc Bay.

Chapter Two

Gen. Tomoyuki Yamashita was probably the most esteemed military commander in the Imperial Japanese Army. Although the dedicated army general had been at odds several times with superiors in Tokyo, such conflicts had not hurt his career. Yamashita was born in 1885 in the small village of Osugi Mura on Shikoku, the smallest of Japan's four homeland islands. As a youngster, he had shown remarkable academic prowess and his wealthy father planned a medical career for his son. However, Tomoyuki had preferred to roam freely among the mountain slopes beyond his village. But he finally went off to the School of the South Seas, an academy for children of noblemen. Here the headmaster had selected Yamashita for the Central Military Academy because of his outstanding academic record. The young agrarian thus began a military career.

Yamashita easily passed all examinations and entered the War College, a school that trained the elite army officer corps. By World War I, he had risen to the rank of captain and between wars he had been assigned to various embassies in Europe. By the 1930s, Yamashita had attained the rank of colonel to command the 3rd Regiment, a key army unit based in Tokyo. During the officers rebellion of 1933, Yamashita had been among the loyalists who crushed the insurrectionists. However, he did not agree with those who wanted severe punishment for the rebels, contending they had acted in good faith. His views had prevailed, but his stand had brought him disfavor among many of the military VIPs.

Still, Yamashita's recognized loyalty and exceptional leadership accelerated his military career. By the eve of World War II, he had become a major general in charge of an army group. His quick conquest of Malaya and Singapore against the British during the early months of the war had earned him the name Tiger of Malaya and won him the esteem of the Japanese people. After this conquest, Yamashita wanted to invade Australia, certain they could easily land on both coasts of the island continent and quickly overcome the meager Australian forces. But, War Minister Hidecki Tojo had disagreed, preferring to thrust westward across Burma and India to link up with their German allies in Asia Minor.

After the Southeast Asia conquests, Tojo had sent Yamashita to Manchuria to command the 2nd Army Corps that guarded the frontier with Russian Siberia. "If war comes with the Russians," the war minister told the Emperor, "you can be assured that Japan's best general will defend this key position on the Siberian border."

For the next two years, Yamashita remained in relative obscurity at his post in Asia. However, in the summer of 1944, Japan realized that the U.S. would soon invade the Philippines. Imperial Headquarters then recalled Yamashita and placed him in command of the 14th Army Group responsible for the defense of the Philippines. Yamashita found about 300,000 troops here, along with 600 aircraft in the 4th Base Air Force, planes that were scattered among dozens of airfields. After he analyzed his resources and his positions at his new station, he did not believe he possessed enough military strength to defend all of the Philippines. Yamashita decided to make his stand on Luzon, the most important island in all of the Philippines.

When the Americans invaded Leyte on 20 October 1944, Yamashita planned to withdraw the bulk of the 25th Army from the island and to build up strong defenses on Luzon. But, Count Hisaichi Terauchi, CinC of all forces in the Southern Region Command of the western Pacific, overruled the 14th Army Group commander and insisted that the Japanese hold Leyte. Even when the Combined Fleet failed miserably in the Sho operation, losing most of its seapower, Terauchi still insisted that Yamashita conduct his major ground war on Leyte.

Yamashita accepted this decision and worked vigorously to carry out a strategy for Leyte. The 14th Army Group commander devised the TA Operation, a plan to send massive reinforcements of men and supplies into Leyte. He quickly sent one regiment of the 1st Division, one regiment of the 30th Division, and some units from Cebu into Leyte to bolster the 35th Army forces already on the island. Although American air units sank several ships, the bulk of these reinforcements successfully reached Leyte. Still, Gen. Sosaku Suzuki was unsatisfied. He said he needed many more troops and supplies to meet the American invasion forces.

Yamashita promised Suzuki that he would take action, so the 14th Army Group commander planned a strategy to send huge reinforcements into Leyte at one time. He called the plan the TA Operation and its success would enable Suzuki to drive the Americans back into the sea. On 1 November 1944, Yamashita called a conference of his commanders at his 14th Army Group headquarters in Manila. In attendance were General Suzuki; Gen. Kyoji Tominga, commander of the 4th Base Air Force in the Philippines; Adm. Akira Shoji, commander of the 1st Transportation Fleet; and Gen. Toshi Mishimura, the 14th Army Group chief of staff.

The conference opened with a mild speech by General Suzuki. He assured the assembled officers that his 35th Army units were holding their positions on Leyte. "Our troops have shown a remarkable resolve. We have completely stopped the invaders' attempt to cross the island and to reach the west coast. We are especially grateful for the reinforcements that have bolstered both the strength and morale of our 35th Army troops. But," he gestured, "we need much more. We need fresh troops in massive numbers and we need provisions that are counted in hundreds of tons. It is not our intent to merely stop the enemy at Leyte, but to drive him back into the sea."

"You must realize, Honorable Suzuki," Admiral Shoji said, "that the Americans now control the waters about the Philippines. And, although the enemy has not yet based many aircraft on the Philippines, his naval planes have flown about the skies in large numbers. So we have been reluctant to send large convoys to Leyte. We have endeavored to sail small fleets at the right time over the right course to avoid enemy detection."

"We need much more," Suzuki insisted.

"Sosaku," General Yamashita said, "we intend to honor your request. That is why we are holding this conference. We have devised a plan to send massive troops and supplies to Leyte in one huge movement. We intend to send the remainder of the 1st Division, the full complement of the 26th Division, and a regiment from the 30th Division in this single effort. These convoys will also include many tons of guns, arms, food, supplies, and even armor to strengthen your army."

"Such an effort could assure victory," Suzuki said.

"But that is not all," Yamashita pointed out. "We plan to send even more reinforcements into Leyte by the end of the month. Even now, two armored regiments are training near Baguio here on Luzon and they will also sail for Ormoc to enhance the strength of the 35th Army."

28

General Suzuki nodded and then looked at Admiral Shoji, the commander of the 1st Transportation Fleet. "Does your fleet have the capacity in marus and warships to carry such large reinforcements to Leyte?"

"It is true that our shipping is limited," Admiral Shoji said, "but most of these new troops will be arriving from Asia in their own marus and escorts. We will only need to supply more warships as escort and a few marus of our own for this operation. It is my understanding that at least a dozen marus and as many destroyers will soon arrive in Manila."

"I see," Suzuki said.

"We will organize these vessels into three separate resupply convoys to sail into Ormoc Bay during the same period," Shoji continued. "The vessels that carry the remainder of the 1st Division, the 26th Division, and supplies for both divisions will sail in tandem convoys out of Manila Bay. At the same time, a convoy will leave Mindanao to carry a regiment from the 30th Division with supplies to Baybay. These convoys will sail as soon as the loaded marus arrive from Asia and we have the routes and time for sailing the vessels. I am inclined to set the arrival dates in Ormoc and Baybay at late afternoon or early evening so we can discharge all cargo and men during the evening hours when we are least likely to suffer American air strikes."

"It is imperative, of course," Yamashita said to the 35th Army commander, "that your shore parties are fully prepared to receive these convoys,

29

discharging troops and supplies quickly, so the vessels may be out of Ormoc Bay as soon as possible."

"I understand," Suzuki said, "and I can assure you, our service units will leave nothing on the beaches by daylight except the egrets that waddle along the seashore." Then the 35th Army commander pursed his lips. "Still, I am somewhat uneasy. We have suffered losses in men and supplies to enemy carrier strikes, especially in the shipping lanes from Manila. Surely, if the enemy learns that three large convoys are sailing to Leyte, will they not make every effort to stop them?"

"Honorable Suzuki," Admiral Shoji said, "we realize as fully as you that we face the danger of enemy air strikes, but we will plan the movement of these convoys very carefully. Our meteorologists predict inclement weather over the Philippine waters within the next few days, with thick rain clouds hovering over the Sibuyan and Camotes Seas for at least a four day period. They also say that besides frequent rain squalls, we may also expect mists over the open sea. Thus, if the marus arrive soon enough from Asia, we will choose this period to move the convoys. If enemy air or submarine patrols are about the area, they will experience difficulty in locating us, much less in attacking us. We may also alter the usual course through the Sibuyan Sea and Masbate Channel to further confuse the Americans."

"I can assure you, Honorable Suzuki," General Mishimura now spoke, "the 14th Army staff has planned carefully."

"Only the best anti-aircraft gunners we can find will man the guns aboard our destroyers and cruisers," Admiral Shoji said. "We recognize the importance of these convoys and the desire for the Americans to destroy them. These gunners have enjoyed considerable success against attacking enemy air units, and I believe they will perform with excellence should the need arrive."

"Let us hope so," Suzuki said.

"We have also taken other steps," General Yamashita pointed again. "We intend to have protective air cover over the convoys at all times."

"That would be reassuring," the 35th Army commander said.

Now, Gen. Kyoji Tominga spoke. "Honorable Suzuki, as you know, we have spared no effort to continue air harassment against the Americans at Tacloban. I will ask the fighter units in the 4th Base Air force to assume responsibility for protecting these convoys. I will ask my air commanders to maintain fighter aircraft over the vessels at all times, operating in relays from dawn to dusk. The 331st Kokutai, whose squadrons are based at Clark Field and Mabalacat, will furnish cover for the two convoys sailing south through the Visayan Sea out of Manila. The 22nd Air Brigade, that maintains its air units on Bacolod and Fabrica Airdromes on Negros, will furnish cover for the convoy carrying the regiment of troops coming northward from Mindanao through the Mindanao Sea."

"But can these air squadrons stop American air units?"

"We know that the Americans are having extreme difficulty in readying their airfields on Leyte for land based bombers," General Tominga continued, "and only a few fighter planes are there now. They would need to send bombers from Morotai and New Guinea, which is quite some distance away. Their naval units have been in combat for many weeks and both their aircraft and carriers need service and supplies, with their pilots spent. We believe, therefore, that we will have ample interceptors to deal with the few aircraft the enemy can spare to attack the convoys."

Yamashita now grinned at General Suzuki. "We have also drawn up a plan to deal with even these limited American resources on Leyte. In conjunction with a 35th Army Drive eastward from the Visayan Mountain Range, we intend to drop an airborne regiment over Tacloban and Dulag to recapture these airfields."

"An airborne operation?" Suzuki questioned.

"For some days we have been mustering transport aircraft at Clark Field," General Tominga said. "We will use a battalion each from the elite 3rd and 4th Raider Regiments to seize and hold these airfield positions, while a battalion from the 4th Regiment also drops at Burauen behind the enemy forces to cut them off. These paratroopers will hold their positions until 35th Army troops link up with them from areas in Central Leyte."

"That is an ambitious plan," Suzuki said, "considering the enemy's strength."

"Thanks to the stalwart defense of the 35th

Army," General Tominga grinned, "I believe this airborne operation can succeed."

Suzuki nodded.

"I have been assured by Count Terauchi that more supplies are on the way to Manila," General Yamashita continued. "I am told that at least three hundred more aircraft, with new pilots and crews, will reach the 4th Base Air Force before the end of November. Imperial Headquarters has agreed to give us all possible help so that we can successfully defend the Philippines. It is our duty to assure Tokyo that we are worthy of such help. We must have faith and determination. Every Nippon son in the Philippines must do his duty to the utmost," the 14th Army Group commander gestured vigorously. "Every officer must inspire the men under him to carry out his role without complaint or carelessness."

The officers at the conference table felt a curious sense of irony in Yamashita's sterling lecture. They knew the 14th Army Group commander had been vehemently opposed to making Leyte the center of defense for the Philippines; that Yamashita wanted to compact his forces on Luzon and other islands in the north to stem the American tide. But when he was over-ruled, he had accepted the decision and then worked vigorously to hold Leyte. Among other things, he had successfully convinced Imperial Headquarters to send the elite 1st and 26th Manchurian Divisions to the Philippines to fight in Leyte. So in this situation, Yamashita had emulated the great Admiral Yamamoto who had opposed the attack on Pearl Harbor but who, when overruled, had planned the 7 December 1941 attacks with ingenious vigor.

When Yamashita finished his short speech, he looked at his watch. "The hour is late. We will retire to the dining room for our meal. May the gods in heaven and our spiritual ancestors give us the strength and wisdom to carry out the TA Operation with complete success."

Thus did the Japanese plan to defeat the Americans in Leyte and in so doing, save the Philippines.

Gen. Walter Krueger, CinC of the American 6th Army, had not shown the optimism of General MacArthur ánd Admiral Nimitz on capturing the Philippines. Krueger had never believed that the seizure of these islands would be an easy task. He had been in the army since World War I when he served as a capable company commander during the St. Mihiel offensive in 1918. By 1926, he had risen to the rank of brigadier general and assumed command of the 63rd Division at Fort Bragg, NC. The division commander had been one of the few ground officers who had agreed with Col. William Mitchell that air power should be more than a supporting service for ground forces; that air power would be a major factor in any future war.

Krueger had been quite dismayed by the court-martial of Mitchell when that U.S. air commander renounced the army brass as incompetent fools who had severely hampered America's military capacity by ignoring the role of the air forces.

Krueger had refused to vote against Mitchell so he himself had fallen into disfavor with some Army VIPs. As a result, by the outbreak of World War II, some 15 years later, he had only risen to the rank of major general.

Fortunately for Krueger, Gen. Douglas MacArthur, who took over command of all Allied Forces in the SWPA in early 1942, considered Krueger an excellent leader who planned well and who worked well with the men under him. So, the SWPA CinC had asked him to command the 6th Army that was primarily responsible for the New Guinea campaigns against the Japanese. Krueger, then at a boring desk job in Washington, quickly accepted and he had shown a remarkable ability in winning victories in New Guinea, the Admiralties, and New Britain. Krueger had then worked with MacArthur in planning the Leyte invasion, but he had insisted that the capture of the Philippines would be a long, hard campaign that would require maximum resources in men, ships, planes, and supplies.

"The Japanese wouldn't give up easily," Krueger told correspondents. "They fought like hell in New Guinea, even in hopeless causes, and they knew damn well that if they lost the Philippines they were on the way to losing the war. I was not surprised when the battle for Leyte turned into a gruelling fight, although even I didn't expect the Japanese to defend the island so vigorously."

Krueger's fears, of course, had come to pass. Despite four heavily armed combat divisions, with three equally armed back up divisions, the Japanese had stopped the 6th Army drive across Leyte. Despite lopsided air victories by U.S. Navy pilots, Krueger's ground troops had made only limited progress.

The 6th Army commander recognized the principal reason for this stalemate—the lack of land based air power in the Philippines. This deficiency had enabled the Japanese to bring reinforcements into Leyte with minimal losses since U.S. Navy planes could not be in all places at all times. Krueger had often thought of Mitchell's warning nearly two decades ago, when the maverick air corps colonel said that air power would be a deciding factor in any future war. In the Pacific, Krueger had seen first hand how air power had turned around the war in New Guinea, the Central Pacific, the Solomons, and the Bismarck Archipelago. He needed such air power now if he hoped to destroy the Japanese on Leyte.

The 6th Army commander had continually complained because 5th Air Force had not yet brought its land based bombers into Leyte, and he committed as many men as he could to ready the Tacloban and Dulag airfields to house the bulk of 5th Air Force planes. When he learned that new Japanese reinforcements had reached Leyte in late October and early November, he was quite perturbed. He called a conference of his Philippine forces at 6th Army headquarters in Tacloban.

Among those at the conference were Gen. Ennis Whitehead, commander of the U.S. Army 5th Air Force; Adm. Daniel Barbey of the 7th Amphibious Fleet, Col. Dan Hutchinson of the 308th

Bomb Wing; Col. Lief Sverdrup, CO of the 28th Air Depot; Army chief of staff Gen. Steve Chamberlin; and a sober faced Adm. Thomas Kinkaid of the U.S. 5th Fleet.

"Both General MacArthur and Admiral Nimitz are furious," Krueger began. "We've been held up badly on all three drives inland. Our airfields aren't yet ready for 5th Air Force bombers, and 5th Fleet is still here instead of sailing back for refueling and reservicing."

"We're doing the best we can, sir," Sverdrup said, "but the job has become almost impossible with this continual rain and those steady Japanese air attacks. We've finally laid steel matting on the Tacloban runway, but we can't accommodate any large number of bombers until we have plenty of hardstands."

"What about the Dulag airfield?"

"We can't keep that strip level long enough to lay steel matting," Sverdrup said. "As soon as we get one day of sunshine, we'll do it. I've told our engineers to work around the clock if such an opportunity comes."

Krueger looked at General Whitehead. "What have we got in Leyte so far?"

"Three squadrons of fighters," Whitehead answered, "and we've been using them as both fighters and fighter-bombers."

"We're ready to fly in bombers as soon as we can," Colonel Hutchinson said. "We've had two B-25 groups and two A-20 groups on full alert for movement to Leyte on a day's notice. In fact, we expect the advance echelons of the 345th and

316th Bomb Groups to reach Tacloban in about a week."

"I must tell you, General, that Admiral Nimitz is even more impatient than you think," Kinkaid said to Krueger. "Our carriers have been out for a long time and so have our surface warships. The 5th Fleet personnel are worn out; we're low on supplies, fuel, bombs, and ammunition. We need relief soon. We didn't expect to be here so long. Land based aircraft should have taken over the air duties by this time."

"We're doing our best, Admiral," General Whitehead said.

"I understand that General MacArthur has been satisfied to simply hold the eastern half of Leyte and contain the Japanese defenders in the hills," Kinkaid said. "It seems like that's been accomplished and our fleet can move out."

"That idea has been discarded," Krueger said. "The enemy is fighting tenaciously in their defenses, and their air units are coming over daily to hit us. While they hold us up, they've been pouring reinforcements into Ormoc, more than a division of men so far. If we don't reach Ormoc soon, they'll have so many men and supplies on this island that we'll never take Leyte."

General Krueger pursed his lips, picked up some papers from his desk, scanned the sheets, and then continued. "General MacArthur, my staff, and myself have come up with a new plan that will expedite both the occupation of Leyte and the cessation of enemy reinforcements. We propose to land troops on the west coast of Leyte below

Ormoc, perhaps in the vicinity of Tabgas on Ormoc Bay.''

"My God, General," Kinkaid cried, "our navy is spent, especially the carrier units. How can you expect the 5th Fleet to support an operation like that?''

'We propose, Admiral, that you simply furnish us with one carrier group for air cover and one battleship group for support," the 6th Army commander said. "Admiral Barbey's amphibious force can handle everything else. We don't expect to make this landing for a few weeks. Meanwhile, perhaps you can send some of the carrier and battleship groups to the rear for resupply and refuel so they can be fully stocked to support the west coast operation.''

The boldness of this plan washed away Kinkaid's anger. He shook his head and then grinned. "Admiral Nimitz won't like this, but we are committed to supporting you in the Philippines. I guess we'll need to postpone the planned naval strikes against Formosa and the home islands.''

"We appreciate that, Admiral." Krueger then looked at Colonel Sverdrup. "It's imperative that we have those airfields ready by the third week of this month. We've got to have as many land based medium and light bombers as possible to fly tactical missions during this operation. We also need at least four fighter groups to contain any air response from the Japanese." He looked at Kinkaid. "Thanks to the 5th Fleet, we won't need to worry about interference from enemy surface warships or carrier units."

Krueger then referred to a map behind him. "I intend to relieve the 24th Division here in the Breakneck Ridge area with the fresh 32nd Division, and we'll relieve the tired 7th Division in the Burauen area with the 11th Airborne Division. We're also planning to use at least one tank regiment and at least two heavy mobile artillery batteries against enemy troops in the hill positions. Such massive attacks will destroy or at least so weaken these enemy units that they cannot interfere with the 77th Infantry and 1st Cavalry Divisions that land on the west coast of Leyte."

"But what about these reinforcements the Japanese keep running into Leyte?" Admiral Kinkaid asked.

"As I said," Krueger gestured, "that's why we need to carry out this amphibious operation as soon as possible. Once we've occupied the Ormoc Bay area, the Japanese will not be able to bring in new troops or provisions. We do know that the enemy usually takes several weeks to prepare resupply convoys so we can assume there won't be any big convoys sailing for Leyte before the end of the month. By then, if all goes well, the 77th and 1st Divisions will have occupied the western shoreline of Ormoc Bay and perhaps the town of Ormoc itself. We'll then have the Japanese 35th Army trapped, with no chance for any help, and we can complete the Leyte campaign."

"I can promise you, sir," Colonel Sverdrup said, "that both the Dulag and Tacloban airfields will be ready for bombers within the next couple of weeks.''

"We'll have our light and medium bomber groups up as soon as Colonel Sverdrup gives me the word," Whitehead said.

"And if we have your carrier group as well," Krueger turned to Kinkaid, "we should have all the air support we need to carry out this operation with minimal difficulty. With four army fighter groups and a few carrier fighter groups we should have plenty of aircraft to stop any kind of air opposition the Japanese throw against us."

"I would say so," Kinkaid answered.

"Okay," Krueger sighed, "let's get with it. Lief," he turned to Sverdrup, "get moving on those runways. I want to see the airfields jammed with 5th Air Force planes by 18 November." He then looked at Admiral Barbey. "Dan, start preparing your amphibious force to load the two combat divisions and all provisions necessary for the landings on Leyte's west coast. And Admiral," he turned to Kinkaid, "I'd like your replenished carrier and surface warship groups back here in two weeks to accompany Barbey's amphibious fleet into Ormoc Bay."

"You'll have them, General."

Thus, the Americans too made plans to break the stalemated Leyte campaign. If the U.S. 6th Army could indeed land a strong force on the island's west coast, Krueger would not only cut off all reinforcements into Leyte, but he could trap the Japanese 35th Army in a pincer movement and effectively destroy them.

41

But Krueger had made a vital miscalculation. He assumed the Japanese would not attempt to land any large reinforcements on Leyte before the latter part of November. However, the elite 26th and 1st Division troops, along with tons of supplies and arms, were on the way to Manila Bay from Manchuria via Southeast Asia. The 30th Division's 14th Regiment, also with plenty of supplies, had already reached Cagayan on Mindanao's north coast, and was waiting for word to leave for Leyte. If these troops and supplies successfully disembarked at Ormoc Bay, the Japanese could maul any attempted landings by the Americans on the west coast.

The Leyte fight could continue for months and thus prolong the Philippine campaign for at least a year.

Chapter Three

On 2 November 1944, the day after the Yamashita conference, Gen. Kyoji Tominga, CinC of the 4th Base Air Force in the Philippines, arose at dawn. By sunup he had eaten breakfast at his Clark Field headquarters outside of Manila. Tominga had been an officer in the Imperial Army Air Force since 1931, when he graduated from the Hiroshima Cadet School. He had been among the few men at the time who believed that air power would decide important battles in future wars, thus supporting rising Adm. Isoroku Yamamoto who had battled those who still believed the infantry and the battleships were the keys to victory.

Young Kyoji Tominga had joined the fledgling air service that had proven itself during the China war in the 1930s. Tominga had built an excellent combat record with six aerial kills and he had shown fine leadership. By the onset of World War II, he was commanding an army air brigade that was supporting the Japanese drive through Malaysia in Southeast Asia. At the end of 1943, he had risen to brigadier general and returned to Japan to work at Imperial Headquarters.

When General Yamashita took over command of the Philippine forces in the late summer of 1944, he had sought out many of his former subordinates for key positions in the 14th Army Group. Among those men he requested was General Tominga who had served Yamashita so well in Southeast Asia. The 14th Army Group commander believed that Tominga had the drive and ability to forge an air force in the Philippines that could meet and defeat the expected American invasion.

Since the American landings on Leyte on 20 October, Tominga's air units had struck hard against the U.S. 6th Army whenever weather permitted. These constant Japanese air strikes had delayed the American completion of the Tacloban and Dulag airfields, so the U.S. 5th Air Force could not bring in its land based bombers and not even enough fighter planes. Thus the 14th Army Group continued to pour reinforcements into Leyte without serious losses.

Tominga was determined to mass as many fighter planes as possible for the TA Operation. When he finished breakfast, he called his aide and drove immediately to the 331st Kokutai orderly room for a meeting with the air group commander, Cmdr. Tadashi Nakajima, who had recently replaced Capt. Rikihei Inoguchi, an air officer now devoting full efforts to organizing and directing Kamikaze air units. Inoguchi had already used such suicide plane units against U.S. warships in Leyte Gulf.

At 0700 hours, when Tominga arrived at the 331st headquarters, Nakajima was already waiting for him. The commander stood rigidly on the wooden step entrance of the frame building and watched Tominga get out of his staff car. The morning sun, already high in the east, shone on the brass buttons of Najkjima's white naval uniform and reflected flashing sparkles. However, a sober look radiated from Nakajima's face for he disliked the idea of an army officer as his superior. He thus reflected the rivalry that had always existed between the Japanese army and navy.

However, the sober faced commander certainly realized that army and navy air units needed to work jointly if they hoped to defeat the enemy. So he had shown the same loyalty to Tominga as he would have shown to a navy admiral.

Cmdr. Tadashi Nakajima had been a veteran airman of the Imperial Navy for more than ten years, having first served as a carrier pilot during the China campaign. By the outbreak of war with the United States, he had served at various naval air bases throughout the western Pacific: the Philippines, Southeast Asia, East Indies, and Rabaul. In early 1942, as a lieutenant commander, he had led the noted Tianan Wing in Lae, New Guinea, where he and his veteran navy pilots had carried on an aggressive and damaging air war against American and Australian units. However, as Allied air forces grew stronger, and with the introduction of the U.S. P-38 fighter plane, Nakajima had seen his Lae Wing disintegrate in size and effectiveness. When the Allies overran Lae, Nakajima had been recalled to Japan to train more airmen.

In mid 1944, Imperial Navy Headquarters had promoted him to full commander and had assigned him as deputy commander in the 331st Kokutai, a naval air group based in the Philippines.

General Tominga smiled as he met Nakajima. "I hope I have not come too early."

"You are always welcome here," Nakajima said. He turned and gestured to an aide. "You will bring tea to my office for me and General Tominga."

"Yes, Honorable Commander," the aide bowed before shuffling off.

Within a few minutes, Nakajima and Tominga sat comfortably in the commander's private office. Nakajima watched the general flip through some papers he had brought with him, but he said nothing. Finally, Tominga sighed and looked at his host.

"Commander, within the next week or so, the 1st Transportation Fleet will send three large reinforcement convoys to Leyte. The Honorable Yamashita believes this must be done swiftly—before the enemy completes his work on the Tacloban and Dulag airfields to base hordes of land based bombers. The Americans have only a few fighter planes on Leyte now, and they must still depend on carrier aircraft to support their efforts. These carrier units are spent and their aviators are exhausted. So, now is the time to strike.''

"So it would seem," Nakajima nodded.

"The plan has been designated the TA Operation," Tominga continued. "I must ask that you prepare two full squadrons of fighters, at least 64 aircraft, to furnish air cover for the convoys that sail from Manila to Ormoc Bay on Leyte's west coast. I have been assured by Admiral Shoji that the antiaircraft gunners of his 1st Transportation Fleet warships are the best."

"I'm sure they are," the 331st Kokutai commander said.

"If the transports and cargo marus have both adept warship gunners and a cover of fighter aircraft," Tominga gestured, "we believe the men and supplies can safely reach Leyte. Two stalwart army divisions will be aboard the marus, the 1st and 26th that have excelled brilliantly in fighting on the Asian mainland. The troops of these units are fresh and eager, anxious to meet the Americans. One regiment of the 1st Division is already in Leyte and doing an excellent job of holding the enemy at Carigara. Still, we have suffered losses in ships during the past ten days, so we can expect the Americans to launch air strikes against this new operation. However, without land based bombers in Leyte, the enemy will need to attack these convoys with fighter-bombers. If the flotillas have good air cover, the Americans cannot effectively interfere with the TA Operation."

Nakajima grinned. "I must tell you, Honorable Tominga, that we have heard of the TA

47

Operation. I anticipated your visit, and I guessed that you would request a special effort from the 331st Kokutai. I have already made tentative plans. We have brought both the 1st and 2nd Fighter Squadrons up to full strength, and we have assigned some of the best pilots to these units. Lt. Makase Ibusuki commands the 1st Squadron and Lt. Muto Yokoyama commands the 2nd Squadron. Both of these men have exceptional combat records and unquestioned leadership qualities. I will keep these squadrons in reserve until such time as you need them."

"Excellent," Tominga nodded. "At the moment, we do not know when these marus will leave Luzon since the convoys have not yet arrived in Manila Bay from Asia. But as I said, we expect the resupply flotillas to leave Manila in about a week. I would ask, therefore, that your two squadrons be ready in two days. These units should operate in relays so that a squadron of aircraft can hang over the convoys from dawn to dusk."

"I concur with your suggestion," Nakajima nodded.

"If possible, I would also like reconnaissance aircraft over the convoy at night," Tomina continued. "We know that the Americans have night bomber units and they could very well attempt to attack the convoys during the dark hours. While your night time pilots may not destroy such enemy units, perhaps your airmen can harass the Americans and drive them off, or at least disrupt their aim."

"I will see that reconnaissance night units are also on duty."

"Good," Tominga answered.

The air force general spent another hour with Commander Nakajima in discussing strategy, drinking tea, and then touring the airfield. Tominga was satisfied. The 331st Kokutai commander had his planes in good condition, his ground crews working diligently, and his pilots on combat ready. Tominga was especially impressed with the 1st and 2nd Squadron leaders, Lieutenant Ibusuki and Lieutenant Yokoyama. Both appeared capable, efficient, and eager. At 0930 hours, the general boarded his special plane and flew off to his next stop—the 22nd Air Brigade headquarters at Bacolod Field, Negros Island.

Capt. Mutohara Okamura, the commander of this army air unit, warmly welcomed Tominga when the general arrived on Negros Island. Since Okamura was also an army officer, he felt none of the subtle resentment of Commander Nakajima, the naval air commander. Okamura first led his general to the officers mess where they partook of a repast of tea, rice cakes, and fresh fruit. The two men then retired to Okamura's 22nd Air Brigade headquarters building.

"I believe I know the nature of your visit, Honorable Tominga," the captain grinned. "It has been rumored that the 1st Transportation Fleet intends to send massive reinforcement convoys to Leyte and they will require strong air support. The reports must be true if you came here personally from Manila."

Tominga returned the grin. "It is surprising how discussions in a secret meeting at 14th Army Group headquarters can so quickly become common knowledge."

"The lowly aides who serve staff officers at such meetings seldom miss an opportunity to bring sensational news to their comrades," Okamura said. "Such aides thereby enhance their standing among their peers."

Tominga nodded. "Then I need only tell you that I have special instructions for your group." The 4th Base Air Force commander again shuffled through some papers in front of him before looking at the captain again. "Mutohara, it will be the duty of the 22nd Air Brigade to protect a convoy from Mindanao that will be carrying elements of the 30th Division and their provisions. We may also need to call on you for air cover over the convoys that leave Manila."

Okamura nodded.

"The Americans have a few fighters on Leyte and the enemy must depend on their spent carrier units," Tominga gestured. "So, now is the time to carry out this action which has been designated the TA Operation—before enemy air strength in Leyte becomes strong. If the convoys have substantial cover, the 1st Transportation Fleet should have no difficulty in discharging troops and supplies."

"I can assure you, General, the 22nd will do its part. Lieutenant Anabuki has some fifty Nakajima (Oscar) fighter aircraft in his 351st Sentai, and Lieutenant Iguchi has an equal number of the new, swift, Mitsubishi J2m (Jack) fighter aircraft in his 352nd Sentai. I have already advised these commanders to have their pilots and aircraft ready for convoy escort duties. To be frank, both Lieutenant Anabuki and Lieutenant Iguchi dislike escorting the Kikusui suicide air units. They have found such duty quite depressing and not really effective."

"Admiral Onishi feels otherwise," General Tominga said, "and he has the authority to carry on this Kikushi suicide missions. But," he gestured, "such missions need not concern us. Your particular duty, as I pointed out, will be to protect the convoy that sails from Mindanao, and possibly the flotillas that sail from Manila Bay."

"My pilots will appreciate such duty," Okamura said. "They will see these convoys and their contents as an opportunity to regain the initiative in Leyte. It is my understanding that the Americans find themselves in a desperate struggle to hold their Leyte gains against determined 35th Army troops. If new reinforcements and their arms can safely reach Leyte, such reinforcements can turn the tide of battle."

"That is the opinion of the 14th Army Group staff," Tominga said. "It is important, therefore, that every man and every pound of provisions from both Manila and Mindanao reach Leyte intact. Commander Nakajima has assured me that his 331st Kokutai will spare no effort in providing aerial cover for the convoys. I hope we can expect the same maximum effort from the 22nd Air Brigade."

"Honorable Tominga, I can promise that we will not allow a single enemy aircraft to get near the marus," Okamura said. He paused and then gestured, "When will this convoy leave Mindanao?"

"We expect the movement in about a week. I would ask that you keep your fighter pilots on full alert as of today. 4th Base headquarters will notify you when to mount aircraft."

Then, as he did at Clark Field, Tominga toured the Bacolod base with Captain Okamura. The 4th Base Air Force commander found the aircraft and airmen here also well prepared. Tominga also met the brigade's two fighter Sentai commanders, Lt. Satashi Anabuki and Lt. Yonosoki Iguchi. He found both men efficient and enthusiastic, traits the two air leaders had no doubt instilled in their pilots. Tominga especially liked Lieutenant Anabuki, a man whose combat record has spanned six years, beginning in China. Anabuki had already downed more than 42 enemy planes, including 19 American planes, since December of 1941.

Dusk had settled over Negros Island by the time Tominga had completed his business with Okamura and completed his jaunts about the airfield. So, the general spent the night in Bacolod and left for Manila the next morning. The 4th Base Air Force commander could report to General Yamashita that four full fighter units would be ready to provide aerial protection for the reinforcement convoys.

On the same morning of 2 November, Gen.

Ennis Whitehead also awoke early in his thatched hut quarters at Tacloban. He had been spending sleepless nights ever since he arrived on Leyte on L-day plus five, 25 October. The 5th Air Force commander had seen his aviation engineers suffer one setback after another in their attempts to ready the Dulag and Tacloban airfields. When heavy rains did not wash away nearly smoothed runways, Japanese bombers put countless holes in the airstrip. Engineers were never ready to lay steel matting. Whitehead prayed for two or three days of sunny weather and at least a day without Japanese air strikes, so he could complete the two airstrips. His Christian God had only half answered his supplications, for engineers had finally laid the steel matting and built more hardstands at Tacloban, while Dulag still remained a sea of mud.

Ennis Whitehead, a USAAF pilot since the early 1920s, had always promoted air power. He had been an excellent leader and by World War II he had risen to brigadier general in charge of planning for the 2nd Service Command of the 4th Air Force in San Francisco. He had shown remarkable ability to get a job done and he had often grumbled because VIPs had kept him inside an office, when he had preferred to do more flying.

When Gen. George Kenney took over the SWPA air forces in August of 1942, the Japanese, especially the Tianan Wing at Lae, had been flying roughshod over Australian and American air units. Kenney had found discipline nonexistent and morale shattered. Kenney's answer to the problem had been Ennis Whitehead, an air commander who was tireless, demanding, and tough. Whitehead had the coldest blue eyes Kenney had ever seen and one stare from his harsh face had prompted subordinates to carry out Whitehead's instructions with no questions asked.

Whitehead had not disappointed Kenney in correcting the problems in New Guinea. The aggressive brigadier moved immediately to the New Guinea battle zone where he lived in tent quarters and ate the same unappetizing bully beef as his airmen. He immediately won the respect of his men, even if they disliked his authority.

By the end of 1942, the forceful Whitehead had turned around the New Guinea air war, boosting morale and directing Allied air units in the maceration of Lae, the astonishing victory in the Bismarck Sea, the destruction of Wewak, the wipe out at Hollandia, the reduction of Rabaul, and the telling East Indies air strikes. When the Americans invaded Leyte, Whitehead had come into the combat zone, against the wishes of General Kenney, the FEAF commander. But Whitehead was determined to get the Leyte air show going as soon as possible, and he felt he could only do this if he himself were on the island.

By this 2 November morning, the 4500 foot air strip at Tacloban had been completed and 54 Lightnings of the 49th Fighter Group's 9th and 7th Squadrons were now based on Leyte as were the 16 P-61s of the 421st Night Fighter Squadron. Thus far, these U.S. units alone were carrying on the exhaustive 5th Air Force operations in the Philippines. However, the P-40s of the 110th Recon Squadron and more P-38s from the 475th Fighter Group were due tomorrow. They would help the 49th and 421st in breaking up enemy air attacks, supporting American ground troops, and hitting supply convoys that came into Ormoc Bay.

Still, Whitehead was irritated. He had heard rumors of the Japanese TA Operation to bring massive reinforcements into Leyte and he doubted if his fighter planes could stop the enemy. He wanted his heavier A-20 light bombers and B-25 medium bombers in Leyte.

After a simple breakfast of powdered eggs, toast, and coffee, Whitehead drove over a muddy road to the 49th Fighter Group headquarters. He found Col. George Walker in his office. The group commander and two officers were drinking coffee and discussing some after action reports.

"Colonel," the 5th Air Force commander called.

When Walker saw the general, he stiffened and cried out, "Ten-shun!"

The two 49th Group officers, Maj. Jerry Johnson of the 7th Squadron and Lt. Col. Bob Morrissey of the 9th Squadron, quickly snapped to attention.

"At ease," the general gestured. After the men relaxed, Whitehead looked at Walker. "How many serviceable planes have you got?"

"At least fifty," Walker said. "Luckily, our losses have been negligible during our interceptor duties over Leyte."

"Not lucky," Whitehead grinned, "good. Your guys are damn good."

True enough! Since the 49th Fighter Group arrived in Leyte on 29 and 30 October, the group had downed an astonishing 57 enemy planes in these few days, including bombers and their fighter escorts that had made strikes on Tacloban and Dulag. On one occasion, the 49th Group pilots had knocked down 12 Bettys and their 14 escorts in a complete wipe out of the attacking force over Tacloban. For these efforts, the 49th had only lost six P-38s which were quickly replaced.

The fighter group had also conducted regular ground support sorties in the battle zones and they had made several fighter-bomber strikes against Japanese shipping in Ormoc Bay. The 49th pilots had sunk two transports, one freighter, and two destroyers on these raids.

Whitehead looked soberly at the 49th Group officers. "I've received some ominous reports. The Japanese apparently intend to send huge resupply convoys to Ormoc within the next week or ten days. We haven't been able to get Dulag ready, so we can't bring in our bombers. That means you'll need to make fighter-bomber strikes if or when these enemy flotillas sail to Ormoc."

"We'll do what we can, sir," Walker said.

"I expect the 110th Recon Squadron to arrive at Tacloban sometime today with their P-40s, and they can help out."

"Yes sir."

"I'm also expecting two squadrons from the

475th Fighter Group to reach Tacloban with at least forty or fifty Lightnings. I've ordered our aviation engineers to work around the clock to make room for them. The 475th will take over interceptor duties while the 49th and 110th will assume the role of fighter-bombers for both ground support and shipping strikes."

"It would be a lot better if we had bombers here, sir," Lieutenant Colonel Morrissey now spoke. "Our pilots are exhausted. The men aren't getting enough rest and our planes aren't getting the kind of service they need."

"I know," Whitehead admitted, "but we've got no choice. You'll need to keep at it until more planes get up here. I've got plenty of air units waiting to come into Leyte. They'll arrive as soon as the Dulag is ready and we expand the Tacloban field."

"Yes sir," Walker said again.

When Whitehead finished talking to Walker, he accompanied the colonel for a stroll through the 49th Fighter Group dispersal area. The general found both pilots and ground crews in excellent spirits and quite optimistic. Since coming to the Philippines they had endured primitive living conditions, harassing Japanese air strikes, and exhausting work hours without complaint. But the 49th Group airmen were quite confident of victory, especially since they had made such lopsided scores against the Japanese.

The 49th airmen had plenty of reason to feel confident. They numbered among their pilots such air aces as Bob Morrissey, Capt. Bob DeHaven,

Edward Dent, Bill Williams, Wally Jordan, Bob Aschenbrener, and the peerless Dick Bong who had attached himself to the 49th Group since returning from the United States. These men had decimated Japanese air units in New Guinea, New Britain, the East Indies, and now in the Philippines. The 49th Fighter Group had scored an astounding 511 air victories over the Japanese since the beginning of the Pacific war.

When Whitehead finished his tour of the area, he ate lunch in the 9th Squadron messhall and then returned to his 5th Air Force headquarters.

By mid afternoon, the 110th Recon Squadron under Capt. Rube Archuleta arrived at Tacloban with 16 P-40s, and ground crews directed the Warhawks into newly prepared dispersal areas. Archuleta soon enough learned that his 110th pilots would fly the very next day. The captain would not even get a chance to acclimate himself to this new environment.

The next morning, the 110th fighter-bombers swept Japanese ground positions in Leyte and during the afternoon the 110th engaged in dogfights over Leyte, shooting down four Oscars without loss to themselves. On the 4th of November Archuleta and his Warhawk pilots attacked barge traffic at Ormoc Bay, sinking several small craft.

Meanwhile, on 3 November, the day after the 110th reached Leyte, Col. Charles McDonald brought his 475th Fighter Group's 432nd Squadron under Maj. John Loisel and the 431st Squadron under the celebrated Maj. Tom Mc-

Guire into Tacloban. On the 4th, the 475th Group fighter pilots engaged in their first Philippine combat when they intercepted a flight of 22 enemy planes which attempted to bomb Tacloban. The Japanese aircraft, under Cmdr. Tadashi Nakajima, suffered near disaster against the pilots of the 475th Group. Only Nakajima and half of his attack force returned safely to Luzon after causing minimal damage on the Tacloban airfield.

Nakajima had been shocked by the swarms of P-38s encountered on this air raid. As he flew home, the 331st Kokutai commander was convinced that the 4th Base Air Force would need to destroy the beehive of U.S. Lightnings at Tacloban before the reinforcement convoys left Mindanao and Manila Bay for the sail to Ormoc Bay.

Although neither Col. Charles MacDonald of the 475th Fighter Group, nor Col. George Walker of the 49th Fighter Group realized it yet, on 5 November, they and their pilots would find themselves in their biggest air fight since the heavy air battles over Rabaul a year ago.

Chapter Four

When Cmdr. Tadashi Nakajima returned from his catastrophic sortie over Leyte, he immediately called on Gen. Kyoji Tominga and Adm. Akira Shoji to meet with him. The two officers agreed and after the evening meal they sat with Nakajima at the 4th Base headquarters in Clark Field.

"I must tell you, Honorable commanders," Nakajima began, "that the Americans have now brought swarms of land based aircraft into Leyte. On our sortie today we met more enemy fighters than ever before and they still had more aircraft on the airfield dispersal areas. The Americans have apparently worked diligently to expand their airdrome so they could bring in many new aircraft."

"How many aircraft would you say they have?" Tominga asked.

"At least a hundred, and perhaps as many as two hundred."

"Were there bombers among them?" Shoji asked.

"We did not see any," Nakajima admitted.

"But, as you know, they often use their P-38s for bombers. We also noted P-40s on the ground and the Americans have been using such aircraft almost exclusively as fighter-bombers."

"Still," Shoji said, "these fighters cannot hurt us as can their bombers. If you are proposing, Commander, that we postpone the movement of the Leyte resupply convoys, such a proposal would be out of the question. The draft for carrying out the TA Operation is all but completed, and the plan will go into effect as soon as the 1st and 26th Divisions arrive in Manila from Asia in the next day or two."

"I would not ask that you delay the operation," Nakajima said, "but I believe we should conduct a huge air strike on Leyte at dawn tomorrow to destroy both these enemy aircraft on the ground and the Tacloban airfield itself. We will thus stop the Americans from launching massive air attacks against the convoys."

"I can agree totally with that suggestion," Shoji said. He looked at Tominga. "Is it possible to launch such a major air strike?"

"Yes," the general nodded, "but you must remember, Admiral, that such an effort will require a large number of aircraft, both fighters and bombers, and we could suffer losses."

"It is a chance we should take," the 1st Transportation Fleet commander said. "I believe that both Admiral Okochi of the Southeast Area Fleet and the Honorable Yamashita himself would concur with Commander Nakajima's suggestion."

Tominga nodded, sighed, and then turned to

the 331st Kokutai commander. "Very well, Commander. You will prepare at least a squadron of fighters and a squadron of bombers from the 331st Kokutai. I will radio Captain Okamura at Bacolod to do the same. You will take off an hour earlier than the 22nd Air Brigade aircraft so you can both arrive over the enemy base at daylight."

"Yes, Honorable Tominga," Commander Nakajima said.

By midevening, the Japanese had prepared units from both the 331st Kokutai and 22nd Air Brigade for attacks on Tacloban the next morning. From the 331st, 24 Judy dive bombers under Lt. Cmdr. Chuichi Yoshioka would leave from Mabalacat, while 26 Oscar fighters under Lt. Makase Ibusuki would take off from Clark Field. On Negros Island, 24 Myrt dive bombers from the 22nd Air Brigade's 353rd Sentai under Lt. Ota Tsubo would leave Fabrica Drome, escorted by 30 Oscars under Lt. Satashi Anabuki. Take off would be at 0300 hours for the Luzon units and 0400 hours for the Negros Island units. Rendezvous would be over Ormoc Bay at 0500, so the formations could reach Tacloban in tandem just at daybreak. Tominga hoped that his 100 plus aircraft would surprise the Americans and knock out most of the U.S. planes on the ground.

Capt. Rikihei Inoguchi, now commanding the 201st Group Kamikaze units, offered to send along a squadron of suicide planes. However, both General Tominga and Admiral Shoji declined the offer. Although they did not say so openly, the two men had frowned on the use of suicide pilots.

Japanese ground crews worked furiously throughout the night at the four Japanese bases. They loaded each Judy with two 550 pound GP bombs and each Myrt, bigger than the Judy, with three 500 pound GP bombs. The 4th Base Air Force ground crews also loaded each Oscar fighter plane with full 7.7mm wing machine gun belts and a dozen wing cannon 20mm shells. By 0300, on schedule, the 24 Judys zoomed off Mabalacat Field. Five minutes later, 26 Oscars from the 331st's 1st Squadron roared off Mabalacat to join the bombers over Manila Bay before droning southeast in the darkness. At 0400, Lt. Ota Tsubo left Fabrica Drome on Negros with his 24 Myrt bombers and moments later, 30 Oscar fighters under Lieutenant Anabuki zoomed off Bacolod Field to join the dive bombers.

By 0500, again on schedule, the 48 bombers and 56 fighters of the 4th Base Air Force rendezvoused over Ormoc Bay, turned east, and headed across Leyte Island for the Tacloban airdrome on the east coast.

At the American airbase, the 5th Air Force now counted 133 fighter planes: 55 P-38s of the 49th Group's two squadrons, 36 P-38s of the 475th Group's two squadrons, 16 P-40s of the 110th Recon Squadron, and 16 P-61s of the 421st Night Fighter Squadron. Whitehead had designated two of these squadrons to remain continually on alert for interceptor duty over Leyte, while the other squadrons would operate as fighter-bombers to support U.S. ground troops or to attack shipping in Ormoc Bay. However, the 5th Air Force commander would need to use most of his fighters this morning to intercept the massive Japanese air formations now droning over Leyte.

At 0520 hours, Lt. Cmdr. Chiuchi Yoshiota, in charge of the Japanese formations, called Nakase Ibusuki. "Lieutenant, you will take your squadron of fighters quickly forward to conduct strafing attacks on the Tacloban airfield and thus thwart any possibility of enemy fighters taking off to intercept us."

"Yes, Commander," Ibusuki said.

Then, Yoshiota called Satashi Anabuki of the 351st Sentai. "Lieutenant, you will bring the fighters of your unit above the bombers to protect us against possible enemy interception. Although we do not expect any such attacks at this hour, we must remain cautious."

"Yes, Honorable Commander," Anabuki answered.

Finally, the 3rd Bomber Squadron commander called Ota Tsubo who led the Myrts of the 353rd Sentai. "Lieutenant, if you study your chart, you will see that the Tacloban runway is along the shoreline and all aircraft are parked on the west side of this runway. I will take my squadron in first to attack any parked aircraft adjoining the airstrip. You will use your sentai of dive bombers to destroy the runway itself."

"We will do so," Tsubo answered.

Then the 4th Base Air Force planes droned over the Visayan Mountain Range of central Leyte and headed toward target.

But the Japanese were indeed naive to believe they could catch the Americans by surprise. Whatever the U.S. 5th Air Force lacked at Leyte, they did not lack a fine early warning system. American radar was exceptionally good and could pick up bogies up to 100 miles away, even planes that skimmed low over the mountain tops. Also, Whitehead had made certain that radar men remained fully alert at their posts during every moment of any 24 hour period. Further, six P-36s of the 421st Night Fighter Squadron maintained a CAP throughout the night, and these Black Widows also had excellent radar. The Japanese formations had barely cleared the mountain range when the P-61 pilots picked up the swarm of bogies on their screens. The American flight leader immediately called 5th Air Force.

"Bogies! A whole slew of them droning eastward. They're about 45 minutes from Tacloban."

The OD officer at headquarters scowled. "How many planes?"

"I don't know, but maybe a hundred of them," the pilot answered. "It looks like they're trying to pull off their biggest raid yet on the Tacloban airfield."

"Okay," the OD officer said. He squinted into the darkness beyond the headquarters hut and then jerked when a radar man turned to him. "I've got the bogies, too, sir; hordes of them."

The OD officer nodded and quickly called the headquarters of both the 49th and 475th Fighter Groups. "Get your pilots out on the double! On the double! At least a hundred enemy planes are heading for Tacloban.''

The night shift at both orderly rooms quickly took action. Within five minutes, ground crews were warming up P-38s, whose machine guns were already fully loaded since the air units were on alert. Other ground crews rousted pilots out of their sacks. So, only minutes after the first bogie reports, 50 or 60 pilots from the two U.S. fighter groups boarded jeeps, drinking coffee on the run, and raced towards their waiting Lightning fighter planes. By 0535 hours, just before daybreak, the U.S. airmen clambered into the cockpits of their planes.

The quick American response portended bad news for the Japanese. The pilots settling themselves into P-38 cockpits were some of the best American aces of World War II in the Pacific: Lt. Col. Bob Morrissey, Lt. Bill Huiseman, Capt. Bill Williams, Maj. Jerry Johnson, Capt. Bob DeHaven, and Maj. Richard Bong of the 49th Group. Among those six men alone, they had scored 125 kills. In the 475th Group, aces like Col. Charles MacDonald, Maj. John Loisel, Maj. Meryl Smith. Maj. Tom McGuire, Capt. Joe Moreing, and Capt. Bob Cline were preparing to take off. These half dozen U.S. fighter pilots had scored more than a 100 victories among them.

The Americans enjoyed two advantages. Their pilots were well trained combat veterans and their P-38s with their 415 MPH speed were better than any fighter plane in the Japanese arsenal.

Soon, in pairs, Lightning pilots raced down the

Tacloban airstrip in an unending parade. For more than 15 minutes, the roar of P-38s echoed across Tacloban. The din had awakened U.S. soldiers and airmen throughout the area, and they hurried to foxholes to wait out the expected Japanese air attack. In San Pedro Bay off Leyte, U.S. sailors donned helmets and life jackets and hurried to shipboard ack ack guns to also await the enemy interlopers.

But few Japanese planes would reach Tacloban.

At 0545, the first band of daylight had brightened the sky beyond Leyte Gulf. In his lead 49th Fighter Group P-38, Lt. Col. Bob Morrissey squinted into the still darkened western sky until he spotted the dark shapes above the mountains. He picked up his radio. "Bandits coming on fast. They look like a vanguard squadron that's heading for Tacloban, probably to make strafing runs. Their bombers can't be far behind them."

"I read you, sir," Capt. Bill Williams said.

Then, Morrissey and his pilots zoomed toward the Japanese Oscars. Dawn had fully emerged now and the U.S. 9th Squadron pilots could see the approaching Japanese 1st Squadron aircraft quite clearly.

In turn, Lt. Makase Ibusuki clearly saw the American P-38s heading toward his formation of Oscars and he gaped in astonishment. He had expected to catch the Americans by surprise. Instead, American interceptors were waiting for him. Ibusuki had no choice but to engage and scatter the P-38s in combat to clear the way for the 3rd Squadron Judy bombers coming after him.

"Prepare for interceptors," Ibusuki cried. "Attack in tight formation."

"Yes, Lieutenant," P/O Arino Kanno answered.

Meanwhile, Lt. Col. Morrissey cried again into his own radio. "Okay, climb high and come down in pairs. No fancy stuff; those Oscars are a lot more maneuverable than our Lightnings."

"Yes sir," Lt. William Huiseman said.

Moments later, the two squadrons clashed just beyond the Visayan Mountains west of Tacloban. But 26 Oscars against 17 Lightnings was no contest. The Americans downed one Japanese fighter after another. Morrissey and wingman Bill Huiseman waded into a trio of Oscars which tried to run. Morrissey pursued two of them and unloosed quick bursts of .50 caliber wing fire and 37mm cannon fire. The 49th Fighter Group deputy commander blew open the cockpit of one plane and knocked off the tail of a second before the two Oscars fell into the mountainous jungles below. Huiseman chopped apart the third enemy plane with withering .50 caliber strafing fire.

Meanwhile, Capt. Bill Williams and his wingman caught another V of Japanese fighters. Williams bagged one Oscar with raking wing fire that set the plane afire before the aircraft arced downward with trailing smoke and crashed into the jungle. His wingman chopped apart the left wing of the second 1st Squadron plane with .50 caliber fire and thumping 37mm shells. The Oscar fell on its back and dropped like a huge stone into the dense terrain below.

Other 49th Fighter Group pilots also scored, knocking down at least six more planes. One Japanese Oscar lost a tail, two of them lost wings, and a fourth lost its engine. The fifth and sixth suffered shattered cockpits that killed the pilots. All six planes plummeted into the jungles below.

Lieutenant Ibusuki and P/O Arino Kanno had scored single kills each. Ibusuki cleverly arced his plane into a sharp turn and unloaded on a P-38 with heavy 7.7mm strafing fire that wrecked the cockpit and killed the pilot. Kanno knocked off the forked tail of another P-38 with exploding 20mm shell fire. The two U.S. Lightnings fell to earth, although one pilot successfully bailed out and reached the lines of the American 24th Infantry Division.

Still, these two kills were small consolation for the Japanese. Ibusuki had lost eleven of his fighter planes to the 49th Group's 9th Squadron and suffered damage to several more. Many of his pilots had panicked after the devastating P-38 attacks and they scattered in several directions.

With the 1st Squadron fighters out of the way, Maj. Jerry Johnson and his fellow pilots from the 7th Squadron roared into the formation of Judy dive bombers. Yoshiota's Judy gunners tried desperately to ward off the American P-38s. However, within minutes, 12 Judys went down and four more suffered serious damage, forcing survivors to turn back.

Jerry Johnson and his wingman dove on a four plane diamond that was hugging the mountain crests to avoid destruction. But Johnson unleashed streaking 37mm cannon shells that struck one Judy squarely. The dive bomber exploded, broke in two, and then fell to earth like two jagged rocks. Seconds later, Johnson scored a second kill when he knocked out the engine on a Judy and the plane wobbled downward and crashed. The major's wingman also downed a Judy when he killed both the pilot and gunner with heavy .50 caliber wing fire.

Capt. Bob DeHaven and Maj. Dick Bong came down in tandem on another quartet of Judys. Within seconds the two veteran American air aces knocked all four planes out of the sky. DeHaven downed one dive bomber when he almost cut the fuselage in half with exploding 37mm shells, and he downed a second when he cut off the tail with heavy tracing fire and more exploding shells. DeHaven watched both planes spin dizzily downward to crash and explode in the jungle, the major's 11th and 12th kills during his Pacific combat career.

Dick Bong quickly finished off his two bombers when he disintegrated the engine of one Judy with 37mm shell fire. He got his second kill when he caught the Japanese plane with machine gun fire which shattered the cockpit. The Judy arced erratically and crashed into the mountains. Bong had thus bagged his 34th and 35th kills in the Pacific, an astonishing record.

The next diamond of Judys fell victim to Col. George Walker, the 49th Group commander, and his wingman, Capt. Elliot Dent. The two U.S. pilots waded into the Judys from above, easily catching the bombers with their speedy Lightnings. The Japanese gunners fired anxiously with 7.7 machine guns, but to no avail. The few bullets that tattooed the American planes had not even slowed down the sturdy P-38s. Walker returned fire with .50 caliber wing guns that sheared away the canopy of a Japanese dive bomber, killing pilot and gunner. Dent hit the gas tank of his victim and the Judy exploded, showering debris throughout the sky. Dent instinctively arced away to avoid damage to himself.

Besides these eight kills, the pilots of the U.S. 9th Squadron got four more Judys and damaged another two dive bombers. Thus less than half of Lt. Cmdr. Yoshioka's planes reached Tacloban. Here, they ran into a skyful of ack ack from both land based army AA gunners and shipboard navy AA gunners. The flak was so thick that Yoshiota and his pilots dropped their bombs haphazardly about the Tacloban airfield, only destroying two P-40s of the 110th Recon Squadron and one P-38 of the 49th Fighter Group. They also damaged two other planes, but punched only a single hole in the runway.

The formations from the 22nd Air Brigade fared no better against the aggressive fighter pilots of the 475th Fighter Group.

Col. Charles MacDonald roared toward the tight formation of Myrts with his 20 P-38s of the group's 432nd Squadron. The colonel and his pilots quickly downed ten of the Myrts with heavy .50 caliber fire and swishing 37mm shells. MacDonald got a Myrt when two exploding shells cut off the right wing and the dive bomber cartwheeled to earth. Maj. John Loisel got two Myrts, his 8th and 9th kills, when he chopped apart one plane with chattering .50 caliber wing bursts, and he destroyed a second Japanese bomber with no less than four 37mm hits that knocked the plane to shreds. Maj. Meryl Smith also got two planes when he dove into a quartet of Myrts like a fox leaping into a hen house. The Myrts tried to scatter, but Smith blew one dive bomber apart and shattered a second before the other two escaped.

Only 14 surviving 353rd Sentai bombers reached Tacloban and these planes also ran into a wall of AA fire from army and navy anti-aircraft gunners. Once more the Japanese dropped their whistling bombs haphazardly, and the attack only gouged two craters in the runway and destroyed another P-40. And even as Tsubo led his Myrts away from target, U.S. AA gunners got one of them when flak blew open the belly of a dive bomber and brought the plane down. Tsubo flew swiftly westward, with only 13 survivors from his 24 planes. Even some of these escapees were badly damaged.

Meanwhile, Tom McGuire took his P-38s of the 431st Squadron after the Oscars of the 351st Sentai. "Okay," the major cried into his radio, "scramble!"

"We read you, Major," Capt. Joe Moreing answered.

Soon, a new dogfight prevailed over the jungles of Leyte. Rattling machine gun fire, thumping shells, and whining engines reverberated across the sky. Below, about Breakneck Ridge, both Col.

Tom Clifford and his men of the U.S. 34th Infantry Regiment and Col. Mitsui Yosuka and his troops of the Japanese 46th Regiment had left their trenches and foxholes to watch the air battles overhead. The Americans continually cheered and the Japanese continually moaned, for the infantrymen of both sides saw Japanese planes continually falling out of the sky. Clifford and his GIs soon lost count of the falling aircraft with the big red balls on their wings and fuselages. Meanwhile, Yosuka and his soldiers counted American victims on one hand.

"Our airmen suffer badly," Maj. Asaeda Shigehara said.

Yosuka squeezed his face. "The American air force grows stronger each day. We must get our reinforcements soon or it will be too late."

"I agree, Colonel," Shigehara said.

East of the ridge, Maj. Ed Edris grinned. "Goddamn, Colonel, our flyboys are giving those Nips a real going over."

"They're cutting them to ribbons," Clifford answered. "It looks like we finally got enough 5th Air Force planes up here." Then, Clifford frowned. "If they can only bring up bombers, especially those B-25s and A-20s. That'd stop any more of these goddamn resupply convoys from reaching Leyte."

"Yeh," Major Edris answered.

Then the two American infantry officers of the 34th Regiment again watched Japanese planes falling out of the sky.

Tom McGuire, who had already scored 31 kills

in the Pacific, surprised a trio of Oscars, tearing two of the planes to shreds before the Japanese even knew the American fighter pilot had pounced on them. McGuire cut one Oscar in half and he knocked the tail off the second before the aircraft plopped into the jungle below. The third plane, piloted by Lt. Satashi Anabuki, adroitly arced away to avoid McGuire's withering machine gun fire and zooming shells. And in fact, Anabuki came down on an unsuspecting victim of his own, shattering the cockpit of the P-38 with 7.7mm wing fire, killing the pilot, before the Lightning spun dizzily downward to crash into the mountains.

However, Anabuki's kill hardly compensated for the heavy losses sustained by the 351st Sentai. Capt. Joe Moreing got a kill when he caught a Oscar that had started to arc away. The exploding 37mm shell tore apart the engine of the Japanese plane that smashed into the highland jungle. Capt. Bob Cline also got a kill when he dove into a formation of three Oscars and got one of them with blazing .50 caliber tracers which tore off the tail. Unfortunately, the other two Japanese planes managed to get away.

The 431st Squadron pilots got three more of Lt. Anabuki's Oscars before surviving Japanese pilots stampeded away. Anabuki could do nothing but muster his pilots and hurry off to the westward.

The surprise raid by the 104 Japanese planes of the 4th Base Air Force had turned into a disaster. They had lost 22 of the bombers and 18 of the fighters, while the Americans lost only four P-38s in the air and another four planes on the ground. The Japanese had left only three bomb craters on the Tacloban runway.

Despite the lopsided losses, Lt. Cmdr. Chuichi Yoshioka brought back glowing reports of heavy American losses. He believed the exaggerated claims of his pilots who said they had left a square mile of destruction at Tacloban, countless planes destroyed in dispersal areas, and many more U.S. aircraft shot down. As soon as he returned to Malabacat, Yoshiota drove to General Tominga's headquarters in Clark Field and told the general that the U.S. airfield at Tacloban had been left in shambles, with most of the parked aircraft destroyed.

"It will take the Americans many days to repair the field and to bring new planes into the base. The resupply convoys should reach Ormoc Bay safely with their troops and supplies before the enemy can intervene with air strikes."

"You are certain of this destruction?" the 5th Base Air Force commander asked.

"Yes, Honorable Tominga," Yoshiota answered.

"I am told that we ourselves suffered considerable losses."

"I regret to say that our casualties were quite heavy," the 3rd Bomber Squadron commander said. "We failed to achieve surprise and hordes of enemy fighters were waiting for us. A great air battle then ensued. We lost over 30 aircraft in the violent conflict. However, our pilots did not lose their resolve and we caused untold destruction.

Thus, their sacrifices were not in vain.''

Tominga nodded. ''I will relay your report to Admiral Shoji so that he can initiate the TA Operation.''

''Yes, Honorable Tominga,'' Yoshiota answered.

At Tacloban, Gen. Ennis Whitehead watched his engineers fill three bomb craters on the runway and replace the twisted segments of steel matting in record time. The men had completed repairs on the apron by the time the P-38s of the 49th Fighter Group and 475th Fighter Group alighted on the airstrip. Whitehead wore one of his rare grins when he greeted Colonel Walker as the 49th Group commander climbed out of his plane.

''Goddamn, George, your guys sure worked over those bastards.''

Walker returned the grin. ''Ennis, we had a very good morning; we knocked down nearly half of their planes.''

A half hour later, Whitehead greeted Col. Charles MacDonald with the same happy grin. ''You and your guys are the best, Charlie, the best. I wish I had been up there with you. Those bitches will think twice before they try another sneak pre-dawn attack on Tacloban.''

''The boys did a good job,'' MacDonald said.

''Good job,'' Whitehead huffed. ''Hell, nobody could have done any better. I'm goddamn lucky to have you guys up here, damn lucky.'' He pursed his lips and tapped his nose. ''Still, I wish I had some B-25s.''

''They ought to have the Dulag runway ready

soon," the 475th commander said.

"I don't know if they can get that field ready before those rumored Japanese convoys head for Leyte. Don't be surprised if you and your pilots double as dive bombers along with the 49th Group and the 110th Squadron."

"If that's what you need us for, we'll be ready," the colonel said.

Whitehead grinned again and tapped Mac-Donald on the shoulder. "Come over to my headquarters, I'll give you a cup of coffee—royale. I've been stashing a bottle of Hiram Walker for a long time and this is as good a time as any to open it."

"I can use a good shot of whiskey," Mac-Donald answered before he ambled off the field with General Whitehead.

Chapter Five

Manila, the large seaport on the island of Luzon, is the largest city in the Philippines. The magnificent buildings, rich architecture, beautiful parks, wide thoroughfares, and clean streets had earned the city the name Pearl of the Orient. The Cavite and Manila Bay harbors had been developed into the best naval bases in the western Pacific, while Clark Field, Nichols Field, and Mabalacat Airdrome, just outside the city, were among the best airfields in the Pacific.

Since occupying the Philippines in 1942, the Japanese had used Manila Bay and Cavite Harbor as staging areas and service depots for distributing men, arms, and supplies throughout the western Pacific. On any given day in these sheltered harbors, hordes of Japanese ships lay at anchor: transport and cargo marus, oilers, service ships, harbor craft, big and small warships, and sub-marines.

Vessels continually steamed in and out of the Manila and Cavite harbors, but the convoy that arrived in Manila Bay on the morning of 7

November 1944 was probably the largest and most important that had ever come to the Philippines. Included in the flotilla were ten huge merchant vessels: 450 foot oiler *Jinei Maru,* 8,000 ton freighter *Akitsushima Maru,* 8,000 ton troops transports *Kamoi Maru, Koa Maru,* and *Kobyo Maru,* and 2,100 ton destroyer transports *Wakatsuki* and *Maki.* This fleet included 10,000 combat infantry troops of the 26th Division along with 6,600 tons of supplies. This fully equipped infantry unit, under the command of Gen. Susumu Nakino, had come from Manchuria to join the Leyte fight.

Also arriving on this 7 November morning was the second element of this huge flotilla: 2,200 ton destroyer-transports *Okimami* and *Hatsuhara,* the 10,000 ton freighter *Koshio Maru,* the 8,000 ton *Noto Maru,* and the huge 10,000 ton troop transports *Kinka Maru, Kozu Maru,* and *Katu Maru.* These vessels carried 6,500 men of the 1st Division's 57th and 58th Regiments, along with 3,000 tons of supplies. These 1st Division troops, under the command of Gen. Tadasu Kotaoka had also come from Manchuria.

Sailors of the Southeast Area Fleet lined the shoreline to watch the array of ships anchor in the bay. These men had seen convoys arrive in Manila before but they had never seen such a large flotilla come in at one time. On the pier stood a group of admirals and generals, while a swarm of Japanese fighter planes loitered above Manila Bay, just in case U.S. naval or army planes chose this hour to attack the harbor. The sight in and around Manila

Bay left the sailors with the sense of awe. The panorama confirmed the rumors that the renowned 1st and 26th Manchurian Divisions had come into the Philippines to fight in Leyte. No doubt, these veterans of the China, Southeast Asia, and Manchuko campaigns would defend Leyte to the death, or more likely drive the Yankee invaders back into the sea.

Both General Kotaoka and Gen. Susumu Makino had achieved enviable records as army commanders. In the 1930s, Kotaoka had spearheaded army units through China and Manchuria in one success after another. He had then commanded the 1st Division in the Malaysian campaign where the sober faced officer had driven British troops southward in reeling retreats, finally capturing two divisions of English soldiers at the surrender of Singapore. Makino had spent most of his time in Manchuria on the Siberian border, where he had constructed excellent defense systems and trained combat troops to discourage any Russian incursions. On two occasions, Makino's troops had routed Russian probing units and the communists had never again attempted to cross the Siberian border.

Of course, one regiment of the Gem Division, the 46th under the veteran Col. Mitsui Yosuka, was already in Leyte. They, along with elements of the Japanese 68th Brigade, had successfully held the line at Breakneck Ridge against the Americans. Surely, when the other Gem Division regiments reached Limon, they would push the enemy back to Leyte Gulf and into the sea.

General Yamashita warmly greeted both General Makino and General Kotaoka when they came ashore. Then, at about 1000 hours, the two newcomers joined Yamashita and other army and navy officers for a conference at 14th Army Group headquarters, where Yamashita discussed the plans for the movement to Ormoc. Among those present besides Makino and Kotaoka were Admiral Shoji, General Tominga, and the convoy commanders, Adm. Matsuji Ijuin, Adm. Muto Matsuyama, and Cmdr. Noriteru Yatsui.

"General Suzuki eagerly awaits the arrival of these troops and supplies in Leyte," Yamashita began. "Such reinforcements of fresh, well supplied troops can change the course of battle. We enjoyed an aerial success yesterday when our brave airmen of the 4th Base Air Force destroyed the enemy's airdrome and most of his aircraft at Tacloban. Thus these convoys sailing to the battle zone should have little or no interference from the American air forces."

"I can assure all of you," General Tominga told the assembled officers, "that fighter units from both the 331st Kokutai and the 22nd Air Brigade will furnish aerial cover during the entire sail to Leyte. With the enemy losses at Tacloban yesterday, the Americans would need to send aircraft from their far off bases at Morotai and New Guinea to attack the convoys, and such a probability is quite remote. While the Americans have done some damage to our shipping from these distant air bases with land based planes, they have not effectively stopped any reinforcements to Leyte.''

After Tominga spoke, Yamashita again addressed those around him. "We hope to have all of these forces into the Leyte battle within the next few days. If you will study the strategy plans in front of you, you will see how General Suzuki proposes to use these reinforcements once they have landed. They will proceed in three columns. The two regiments from the 1st Division will move swiftly to Limon to join the 68th Brigade and the other 1st Division regiment at Carigara. These forces in the north will then launch massive attacks against the Americans to drive them back to Tacloban. These northern forces will then occupy the enemy's airfield at Tacloban, while driving his troops into the sea.''

"I understand," General Kotaoka said, scanning the sheet in front of him.

The 14th Army Group commander nodded and then continued. "On the second page of these plans, you will see that all three regiments of the 26th Division will join the 16th Division and 102nd Division troops at Barauen in central Leyte. The heavily strengthened force will then drive eastward along the Marabang River to the east coast of Leyte. They will capture Dulag and thus cut off American units to the south from their forces to the north.''

"We will not fail, Honorable Yamashita," General Makino promised.

"The 14th Regiment that sails from Mindanao will disembark at Baybay, south of Ormoc and then march overland to join General Fukue's forces that are now engaging the enemy west of Abuyog. With these fresh troops and supplies, General Fukue in the southern sector will be strong enough to drive eastward and recapture Abuyog."

"This plan is a wise one," General Kotaoka said.

Yamashita nodded and then looked at Akira Shoji of the 1st Transportation Fleet. "Admiral, you may now explain the movement of these convoys."

Shoji nodded, rose from his chair, shuffled through some papers, and then looked at the officers. "You all know the importance of the TA Operation. It will be our most intense effort yet to bring reinforcements to Leyte. I would have preferred to sail these convoys at the same time, but the unloading facilities at Ormoc are limited. So we have planned a schedule so that the convoys which leave Manila Bay will arrive at Ormoc on two successive late afternoons or early evening. Convoy One that carries the 1st Division will leave Manila Bay tomorrow morning, 8 November, to reach Ormoc on the late afternoon of 9 November. The esteemed Admiral Ijuin will command this convoy." He looked at Matsui Ijuin. "Admiral?"

Ijuin nodded and referred to some notes in his hand. This convoy commander had been in the Pacific war for more than two years, serving as both an escort commander and a desron battle fleet commander. He had been successful most of the time, but he had suffered defeat during the Bougainville campaign in November of 1943, when the Omori fleet had been mauled by an American battle fleet in the night battle of Empress Augusta Bay. In fact, Ijuin's own destroyer had been sunk, but he had been luckily rescued after the Empress August Bay defeat. Ijuin had escaped the scathing reprimands or loss of command as had befallen other naval officers in that battle. But perhaps his dramatic rescue from the sea or his influence with the then Combined Fleet CinC Admiral Koga had spared him from disgrace.

"We will be carrying the regiments of the 1st Division and a few supplies aboard the four transport marus and two destroyer-transports," the Convoy One commander said. "The cargo vessel *Koshio Maru* will carry most of the provisions. I will lead this convoy in light cruiser *Kumano*. We will also have five destroyers including the passenger warships, and four Koshii coastal defense vessels as escorts. The gunners aboard these ships are the best in the Southeast Area Fleet, and they will deal successfully with enemy aircraft should such aircraft attempt to attack us. Further, since we will also have strong air cover, I have every confidence that the troops and supplies of Convoy One will reach Ormoc safely. I was told that shore parties at Ormoc will labor tirelessly to quickly unload these men and supplies."

"Good," Admiral Shoji nodded. He then looked at Adm. Muto Matsuyama the veteran of the

Solomons campaign. Matsuyama had been on the staff of Adm. Raizo "Tenacious" Tanaka, who had been so successful in his Tokyo Express runs during the Guadalcanal campaign. Matsuyama had also been effective in evacuating troops from the Marshall Islands during that losing campaign, and he had successfully withdrawn troops from the Palaus Islands during this last battle before Leyte. Thus, because of Matsuyama's extensive experience in transporting troops, Shoji had placed him in command of the second large flotilla, Convoy Three. "Muto, are you prepared to sail?"

"Yes, Honorable Shoji," Matsuyama answered. "We will have the full 26th Division aboard the large transports *Kamoi, Koa, Kobyo Marus* and the two destroyer-transports *Wakatsuki* and *Maki*. These vessels will also carry some of the provisions, but most of the supplies are aboard cargo *Akitsushima Maru*. We will also have the oiler *Jinei Maru* in our flotilla. Five other destroyers and two coastal defense koshiis will compose the escort. The anti-aircraft gunners aboard these vessels are exceptionally accurate, for they have been hand picked. Still, we welcome the Honorable Tominga's promise to provide air cover as added safety. I anticipate no problems in landing these troops and supplies at Ormoc."

"Your convoy will leave Manila Bay on the morning of 10 November," Shoji said, "and you should arrive at Ormoc on the late afternoon of the 11th. By then, the shore crews will have completed their disembarkment of troops and supplies from Convoy One, and they will be ready to discharge the men and provisions of Convoy Three."

"I will arrive on time," Matsuyama promised.

Admiral Shoji now looked at Cmdr. Noriteru Yatsui, who had flown up from Mindanao in an Emily flying boat to attend the meeting. "Commander," the 1st Transportation Fleet commander said, "while Convoy Two is the smallest of the three flotillas, it is no less important. The men and supplies aboard your two large marus must reach Baybay to reinforce the tired men in General Fukue's forces which are also low on supplies."

"Yes, Honorable Shoji."

"Your convoy will leave Cagayan Harbor on Mindanao's north coast on the morning of 10 November so you can reach your destination by the evening of the 10th. I have been assured that shore parties will be ready to disembark your troops and to unload your supplies. The soldiers of the 14th Regiment will then join the troops beyond Baybay by the evening of the 12th."

"We will spare no effort," Commander Yatsui promised.

Thus, the Japanese finalized their plans to send the three resupply convoys to Leyte. And indeed, if Yamashita could land on Leyte these 20,000 plus troops and some 10,000 tons of supplies and arms, the Japanese might well break the stalemate on that island and send the American GIs reeling in full retreat. The U.S. naval airmen needed rest, and the 5th Air Force pilots at Leyte were also tired. The 49th Fighter Group pilots, especially, had been straining to the limit of their endurance in continual efforts to intercept Japanese bombers, support, ground troops, indulge in dogfights, and occasionally attack Japanese shipping off Leyte's west coast. But worst of all, while P-38s and P-40s might damage the TA Operation convoys, these U.S. fighters were not likely to cause many losses. The Americans needed much heavier aircraft, the low level light and medium bombers, to really hurt the Japanese. But, at the moment, there was not a single U.S. 5th Air Force bomber in the Philippines.

At Tacloban, Gen. Ennis Whitehead and his air commanders of 5th Air Force on this same morning of 7 November met in his headquarters. Among them were Col. Charles MacDonald of the 475th Fighter Group, Col. George Walker of the 49th Fighter Group, Capt. Rubel Archuleta of the 110th Recon Squadron, Col. Dan Hutchinson of the 308th Bomb Wing, Col. Lief Sverdrup of the 28th Air Depot, and Gen. Steve Chamberlain, the 6th Army chief of staff.

"First, I'd like to thank the fighter pilots for their excellent job against Japanese air units which tried to attack Tacloban," Whitehead said. "Unfortunately, we can't assume they won't try new raids. Despite their heavy losses, they aren't likely to give up. We'll need to remain on alert for more possible donnybrooks over Tacloban. However, an even more pressing problem is this rumored Japanese reinforcement convoy. Filippino guerrillas in Luzon report that a large flotilla of warships, cargo ships, and troops transports arrived in Manila Bay this morning. So, the rumors seem valid."

"When do you expect this convoy to sail for Ormoc Bay?" MacDonald asked.

"We don't know," the 5th Air Force commander said. "But, we'll keep recon units over the Sibuyan Sea and Mesbate Channel to keep an eye out." He looked at some papers in his hand. "I've called you here to outline specific asignments for all air units in Tacloban, including ground support, because General Krueger is especially anxious to break the stalemate."

"As you know, Ennis," General Chamberlain now spoke, "we've run into stiff opposition on all fronts. Units of the 24th Division at Breakneck Ridge are fighting for every yard in their attempt to reach Limon, and they need more air support if they hope to overrun the Japanese defenses. Navy carrier units are spent, so the burden must fall on 5th Air Force."

General Whitehead looked at Archuleta. "Captain, I'm going to assign your P-40 squadron strictly to air support for the 24th Division at the Breakneck Ridge area. A liaison man from Col. Tom Clifford's 34th Regiment is coming in this evening and we'll send him to your headquarters. I'd like you to assign one of your own men to him so they can coordinate air strikes in that area."

"Yes sir," Archuleta said.

Whitehead now looked at Colonel MacDonald. "Charlie, the same thing applies to your P-38 squadrons. I want your 432nd Squadron to give continual ground support to the 7th Division units at Burauen in the center, while your 431st Squadron supports the 96th Division units to the south beyond Abuyog. We must break the enemy defenses in these areas to reach Leyte's west coast."

"Yes sir," the 475th Group commander answered.

"Colonel Logie of the 32nd Regiment at Burauen and Colonel Laya of the 383rd Regiment at Abuyog will also send liaison officers to your group headquarters this evening," General Chamberlain said. "You're to assign a man from each of your squadrons to work with them in coordinating group support."

"We'll have a couple of good men ready," MacDonald promised.

Whitehead now looked at Colonel Walker. "Since the 8th Squadron of your group will arrive today, we'll use all three squadrons from the 49th Group as interceptors against any new Japanese air attacks. I'm also expecting a couple of squadrons of P-47s from the 348th Fighter Group to arrive in Tacloban in a couple of days. That should give us plenty of firepower to deal with Japanese planes trying to attack the Tacloban and Dulag airfields."

"But what about the big Japanese resupply convoy," Colonel Walker asked.

"If or when recon planes spot these rumored convoys coming through the Sibuyan Sea or Mesbate Channel, we'll suspend all other operations and launch fighter-bomber attacks. All of you should be prepared for such missions."

"What about the bombers?" MacDonald asked. "When will they get here?"

"We've almost finished the Dulag runway," Colonel Sverdrup now spoke. "If this good weather holds for the rest of the day, we'll have steel matting down by tonight. Then we can start bringing in bombers."

"The 345th Group's B-25s are waiting at Biak, fully packed, and ready to move," Colonel Hutchinson said. "They'll be sending a flight of B-24s up here tomorrow to try out the Dulag strip. If all goes well, we'll bring in the rest of the group within a few days. The 312th Group has been at Hollandia for months, but they're also ready to move their A-20s to Leyte. Their advance echelon should arrive in the next day or two, and their planes ought to be here within ten or fourteen days. The 417th Bomb Group will also arrive in Leyte within the next couple of weeks with their A-20s."

"As soon as we have these two light bomb groups and the medium group up here, we'll be in good shape," General Whitehead said. "The A-20s and B-25s will be used for ground support and shipping strikes in Ormoc Bay. That should take some of the pressure off the fighter units."

None of the air commanders answered.

"Okay," Whitehead sighed, "get back to your units and relay these various assignments to your squadron and flight leaders. Meanwhile, I'll tell Admiral Kinkaid that we'll need naval air support for another couple of weeks. He won't like it, but he really has no choice."

Far to the south, at Biak Island off New Guinea's northwest coast, and 900 miles from Leyte, Maj. Glen Doolittle had just landed after a B-25 strike on Manado in the Celebes, East Indies. By dusk, the 498th Squadron commander of the 345th Bomb Group was in his orderly room with Capt. Bill Decker.

"Goddamn, Glen, another dead horse mission," Becker complained. "When the hell are we going to get some good targets again, maybe some of that shipping up in the Philippines?"

"We'll be moving north pretty soon," Doolittle answered. Then the major grinned. "You and I are going to Leyte tomorrow with a small advance flight. We may get a chance against shipping targets sooner than you think."

"It can't be too soon for me," Decker said.

Across the bay at Noemfoor Island, Maj. Bill Dunham of the 348th Fighter Group's 460th Squadron sat in the officers mess sipping coffee with Lt. Tom Sheet and Capt. Henry Fleischer. They had just returned from a fighter-bomber sweep over Babo Airdrome in western New Guinea, where they had found only wrecked planes on the ground. Countless air attacks in this area had left the Japanese base in ruins, and U.S. airmen now considered a mission to Babo as nothing more than a boring routine.

"The Philippines," Fleischer gestured, "that's where the action is. The 49th Group is tangling with Nip fighters every day of the week, and hitting shipping at least every other day. They're

91

the ones who are really in this war."

"We who engage in mop up operations also serve," Dunham grinned.

"Mop up!" Lieutenant Sweet growled. "Christ, all we're doing is strafing smashed planes, wrecked buildings, and pulverized airstrips. We haven't seen a Japanese interceptor for weeks. All we get are a few barges once in a while because the Nips won't send as much as a small Sugar Charlie to New Guinea or Amboina anymore."

"We'll be in the Philippines soon enough," Dunham said. "Drink your coffee."

"Ah, hell," Sweet gestured in disgust.

Up the New Guinea coast, at Sansapor, Maj. Bill Cowper of the 18th Fighter Group's 70th Squadron stood on the field on this 7 November day and squinted at his P-38s in their revetment area. Next to him stood Lt. Bob Mitchell. They had been on another escort mission today during a bomber strike against Amboina in the East Indies. But, as usual, they had not met a single enemy interceptor, while the B-25s bombed an already rubbled base.

"All we do is take plane rides," Mitchell moaned.

"I guess," Cowper answered. "But they want the Indies totally flattened."

"Goddamn, there's nothing left to flatten," Mitchell complained. "When the hell are we moving up to the Philippines?"

"I don't know," Cowper said, "but I'm told we'll soon be escorting B-24s to hit airfields and shipping in and around Mindanao, Negros, and

Palawan. We're sure to run into enemy interceptors on those missions."

"I'd sure enjoy a good donnybrook," Mitchell
sighed. "It's been so long."

Some 300 miles to the north, at Morotai Island,
Col. Ed Gavin, commander of the 38th Bomb
Group, sat in his shack with his squadron
commanders: Maj. Ed McClean, Maj. Ed Maurer,
Lt. Col. Ed Hawes, and Capt. John Irick. Gavin
had assumed command of the 38th only a couple
of weeks earlier, having taken over from the very
popular Lt. Col. Howard Pequin. Gavin, a
veteran pilot who had mastered skip bombing
tactics, had been training B-25 crews in this
technique with Col. Carl Brandt, commander of
the Replacement Training Command in the
SWPA.

Skip bombing, first used in the Bismarck Sea
battle some 1½ years ago, had enabled B-25s to
truly hurt Japanese shipping. So, General Whitehead had asked Colonel Brandt to train most of
the new B-25 replacement crews in this technique.

Skip bombing tactics combined the use of
delayed fuse bombs and ten forward firing
strafing guns. In the SWPA, the medium B-25
bomber had been modified into a so called
commerce destroyer that was especially designed
to attack shipping. Technicians had removed the
standard bombardier compartment in the nose
and installed six .50 caliber machine guns, with
two more guns each on either side of the forward
fuselage, ten guns in all. Then, in place of
standard bombs, ordnance men loaded the B-25

with two to four 500 pound five or ten second delayed fuse bombs. Thus, the Mitchell could attack a ship at masthead height and drop its bombs within an astonishing 50 to 100 yards of target, raising dramatically the possibility of a hit. The delayed fuse on the bomb enabled the B-25 to arc away safely from target before the explosion.

The commerce destroyers worked in pairs. The first pilot went in with heavy strafing fire to clear the deck of AA gunners, and the second B-25 followed to drop skip bombs with minimal interference from the ship's crew. Then, the B-25s reversed their roles. The first skip bombing pilot now came in to fire strafing guns, while the earlier strafing pilot followed to drop his skip bombs.

Col. Ed Gavin and his 38th Bomb Group crews knew of the heavy Japanese shipping around Leyte and they were hoping to get a chance to attack such enemy vessels in Philippine waters. But they had received no word yet on moving to the Philippines.

As these 38th Group officers sipped coffee, Major McClean looked at Gavin. "When are we moving north, Colonel? I hear the Japanese have been sending a parade of resupply convoys to Leyte. We could sure do a job on them with skip bombing tactics."

"I don't know," Gavin answered, "not until they've got the airfields on Leyte ready for us, and maybe not until they've cleared the air of Japanese bombers over Leyte."

"Then we may never move," Major Maurer scowled. "From what I hear, the Japs have an inexhaustible supply of planes in the Philippines, including those suicide planes that have been hitting our navy ships."

Gavin sighed. "I can only wait for orders. Meanwhile, we'll continue to hit targets in the Halmeharas, Amboina, and the Celebes. Please prime your crews for a mission tomorrow to Bitjoli in the Halmeharas. We'll have briefing at 0600."

"Yes sir," Ed McClean answered with a tinge of disgust.

No doubt, the U.S. airmen at Biak, Noemfoor, Sansapor, and Morotai felt an envy for the combat crews now in the Philippines. Those airmen up north were in the real war, making strikes on plump shipping, hitting fat targets in the ground war, and brawling with Japanese air units in regular dogfights, where the enemy usually lost by a lopsided score.

However, conditions would change abruptly for Maj. Glen Doolittle of the 345th Group, Maj. Bill Dunham of the 460th Squadron, Maj. Bill Cowper of the 70th Squadron, and Maj. Ed Gavin of the 38th Bomb Group. Within the next two or three days they would become part of the biggest aircraft strikes against ships since the Battle of the Bismarck Sea. Further, the stakes in this battle would be extremely high for U.S. forces—the conquest or the loss of Leyte.

Chapter Six

No doubt, the TF 38 U.S. Carrier fleet was spent. The carriers had been operating continually at sea since the aerial sweeps over Formosa on 10 October. Since then, they had made attacks on Okinawa, Iwo Jima, and then the Philippines. Not only were the flattops low on fuel and supplies, but also low on ammunition. So, on the evening of 7 November, Adm. Fred Sherman, in temporary command of the TF 38 force, sent a message to 5th Air Force in Tacloban.

"Retiring to Saipan for refueling and resupply. Will return to Leyte waters in seven to ten days to support Ormoc landings."

General Whitehead accepted the departure of TF 38 without complaint. He knew the U.S. carriers had been too long at sea, and they needed to replenish themselves before the supporting missions for the amphibious operation on Leyte's west coast. Whitehead agreed with General Krueger that a back door landing in Ormoc Bay would not only break the ground war stalemate in Leyte, but also give him breathing room to expand his Tacloban and Dulag airfields, and to even develop the Abuyog field to the south. Shortly after the departure of TF 38, Whitehead met with Gen. Walter Krueger, 6th Army chief of staff Steve Chamberlain, and 308th Bomb Wing commander Col. Dan Hutchinson.

"Ennis," Krueger said, "I know the temporary retirement of the TF 38 force places a heavy burden on your 5th Air Force, but your airmen will simply need to make a special effort; perhaps fly combat missions at an accelerated pace for the next week or two."

"We've already met with group commanders to make special assignments to each unit," the 5th Air Force commander said. "All squadrons have a specific task, either supporting ground troops, hitting shipping in Ormoc Bay, or intercepting Japanese air units which try to bomb our airfields."

"Good," Krueger nodded. He shuffled through some charts on his desk before he spoke again. "I don't expect your fighter units to break the stalemate on Leyte, but, until the carriers return, it's imperative that they at least help us to hold the line and stop some of those Japanese resupply convoys."

"Fortunately," Colonel Hutchinson now spoke, "we've laid the matting for the Dulag strip. A flight of B-25s from the 345th Bomb Group is flying in. If the field is satisfactory for them, we'll bring the entire 345th Group in, and perhaps one of the A-20 light bomber groups ahead of schedule. That should give us considerable firepower. Meanwhile, we'll make do with the P-38s, P-40s, and P-61 night fighters we have here now. We'll use them as interceptors as well as fighter-bombers."

"I guess that's all I can ask," Krueger said.

Meanwhile, aboard *USS Essex,* the flagship of TF 38, Adm. Fred Sherman stood on the bridge with AG 4 commander, Cmdr. Jim Mini.

"We've got a CAP over the task force as you requested, sir," Mini said. "We don't expect Japanese aircraft out here in the middle of the Philippine Sea, so the aircraft will concentrate on the possible presence of submarines."

"Good," Sherman answered.

"Are we going to Ulithi, sir?" Mini asked.

"No," Sherman answered. "Only Admiral Bogan's TG 38.2 is going there. His group is extremely low on fuel and supplies. But, Admiral Davison will join us with his replenished TG 38.4 sometime today, and our other two groups will fuel at sea before we continue on to Saipan for more arms and ammunition."

"Aye sir," Mini answered. He then squinted to his left where he could see the other carriers of his TG 38.3 group, *USS Langley* and *Ticonderoga.* Mini appreciated the return to Saipan where he could stand on dry land for at least a few days, eat a good meal in the base messhall, and escape the continuous motion from a rolling sea.

Behind TG 38.3, the carriers *USS Hornet, Monterey,* and *Cowpens* of TG 58.1 sailed in tandem, with destroyer and cruiser escorts at their sides. The *USS Wasp* had left the group earlier, sailing to Guam to pick up a new air group. The *Wasp* airmen had worked strenuously during the Luzon and Formosa strikes that left only 30 pilots out of 113 fit for duty. So, the carrier needed a new air group before she could return to action.

In the #2 ready room of *Hornet,* Lt. Cmdr. Bob Farrington sat with Cmdr. Frank Schraeder, the AG 11 commander. The two torpedo bomber pilots were tired, for they had been at sea for more than two months. Farrington sipped coffee, while Schraeder checked over some maps in front of him.

"You don't need to do that now, Frank," Farrington grinned. "We're on our way to the rear for some rest; and I can sure use it."

Schraeder returned the grin. "I always like to know where I've been and where I'm going. When I brief pilots and crew, I need answers for them."

Farrington only sipped his coffee again and squinted out of a porthole window at the rising crests of water. "The sea is getting a little rough. I'm glad we're not going out today."

"We've been out enough for a while."

Farrington nodded. He had been in the war for more than 12 months. He had been among those pilots who had made the first carrier strike on Rabaul almost a year ago, and he had been attacking Japanese surface ships and island bases ever since. Twice the enemy had shot him down and twice PBYs had rescued him. The torpedo bomber leader was expected to be relieved soon, and he hoped to be home for Christmas. He squinted still again at the sea beyond his porthole and he then looked at Schraeder.

"Where are we going next, Frank?"

"Probably to Luzon to soften up the place for new ground troop landings."

"You think they're going to invade Luzon?"

"You can bet on it," Schraeder answered.

Bob Farrington did not answer. He sipped his coffee again. He was glad he was going to Saipan for a rest.

In the #3 messhall of *USS Monterey,* Lt. Cmdr. Ron Gift and Lt. Tom Driess, two torpedo bomber pilots of AG 28, sat at a table and drank coffee. Driess stared out of a porthole and watched the sea grow steadily more rough.

"Looks like we're on the edge of some kind of storm."

"They think it might be a typhoon," Gift answered. "That's why we're taking a roundabout course to Saipan. I just hope to hell we get there before that damn storm gets too far north."

"Ron," Lieutenant Driess said, "how long do you think we'll stay on Saipan? Christ, I'd like to keep my feet on dry land for a while."

"At least a week," Gift said.

Driess grinned. "I'd like that; a real vacation."

The two *Monterey* airmen had been in the Pacific carrier war for more than a year, having first seen action during the northern Solomons campaign, and then the Gilbert campaign. In early 1944 they had participated in the Marshall Islands and Truk air strikes, and then the Battle of the Philippine Sea in June. Gift and Dreiss had scored heavily against Japanese shipping, climaxed by the heavy damage to a large Japanese carrier.

After a brief rest at Saipan, *Monterey* had returned to action in support of the Philippine invasion. The carrier's airmen had conducted strikes on Formosa, Okinawa, Luzon, and Leyte itself before the landings. Gift and Driess had participated in two torpedo bombing attacks on shipping in Manila Bay, where heavy AA fire and Japanese interceptors had shot down three of *Monterey's* Avengers.

No doubt, this duet of naval pilots needed rest. Between them, they had flown 121 sorties during the past month.

"I hear they got steak on Saipan," Dreiss grinned, "with fresh spuds and vegetables. I can't wait."

"We'll be in Saipan soon enough," Gift said. "Meanwhile, enjoy your coffee and thank the good Lord we won't fly combat missions for the next week or two."

"I'd sure appreciate that," Dreiss said. Then he frowned. "Ron, where do you think we'll go next?"

"Who knows," Gift shrugged. "There's so many goddamn targets in the western Pacific, they'll likely send us anywhere."

"Yeh," Dreiss nodded. He squinted again through the porthole. The swells seemed even higher now, and he could see carrier *Hornet* rolling more intensely. The torpedo bomber pilot hoped they reached Saipan soon, before the sea turned into a maelstrom.

A hundred miles southeast of these two carrier

groups, TG 38.4 steamed at a comfortable 24 knots to make its rendezvous with the TG 38.1 and TG 38.3. Carriers *USS Franklin, Enterprise, San Jacinto,* and *Belleau Woods* of TG 38.4 had been in combat for over two months, culminating with a two week support mission at Leyte. The TG 38.4 pilots had continually fought off Japanese fighter and suicide planes, while its dive bombers and torpedo bombers had attacked enemy defenses on land and surface ships at sea. The aircraft of Admiral Davidson's carrier group had also conducted attacks on shipping and airfields in the Visayas, Luzon, Cebu, and Palawan. By late October, the group's pilots were utterly spent and the ships almost out of ammo and supplies.

Admiral Sherman had ordered TG 38.4 back to Ulithi to rest the airmen for a few days, while shore crews filled magazines and supply lockers. Now the carriers would join the other TF 38 groups for the sail to Saipan where they would stand by to await their next assignment.

In the officers rec room of *USS Franklin*, Lt. Cmdr. Bob French ate a soft roll that had just come fresh from the galley. Next to him, Lt. Charles Skinner also ate a roll and drank coffee. The two torpedo bomber pilots had seen continual action during the past two months and they appreciated the return to Ulithi for rest. French had bagged himself a transport in the Sibuyan Sea during the opening days of the Leyte campaign, and Skinner had sunk a coastal defense ship in the same air attacks on 27 October.

"Larry, when do we rendezvous with the other

carriers?'' Skinner asked the TSB 13 commander.

"About noon," French answered. He squinted through the porthole at the heavy swells. "It might be longer in these rough waters."

"I don't understand this," Skinner shook his head. "We just left Ulithi and now we're going to Saipan. I thought we'd be heading back to combat."

"Don't complain," French grinned. "We've been in this goddamn war for over a year and I'll take all the rest I can get. The base at Saipan has nice soft beds in the barracks, good food, a sandy beach, and a good recreation area. That's okay by me."

"Do you think we'll go back to Leyte?" Skinner asked.

French shook his head. "Army planes will be supporting the Leyte battle from now on, so I hear. So they won't need us. My guess is we'll hit Formosa and Luzon again."

Then a sudden burst of AA fire jerked the two men. Skinner scowled. "Another goddamn Emily recon plane. Christ, they're a long way from home."

"Well, they can't dog us much longer," French answered. "We'll soon be out of range for even those long range Nip flying boats. Relax," the TSB 13 commander grinned. "Think of that nice soft bed on Saipan."

"Yeh," Skinner answered with a grin of his own.

By noon, despite the rough sea, TG 38.4 rendezvoused with TG 38.1 and TG 38.2 on schedule.

Here, the groups loitered while oilers topped off the fuel tanks of the carriers, a chore that took more than two hours in the heavy swells. Then, at midafternoon, TF fifty-eights three carrier groups maneuvered into formation. Then with cruiser and destroyer escorts, the flattops sailed eastward at a leisurely 20 knots. The slow speed enabled the ships to conserve fuel and to mitigate the rolling motion of the heavy seas.

At 1500 hours, 7 November, Japanese observers aboard one of the Emily flying boats radioed 4th Base Air Force headquarters in Clark Field. "The enemy carrier force is now 300 miles east of Leyte, obviously sailing for Saipan. You may initiate TA Operation without fear of attacks from the enemy's naval aircraft."

"Good news," the OD officer at Clark Field answered. "Both General Tominga and Admiral Shoji will be glad to hear this."

But, Cmdr. Jim Mini of *Essex,* Lt. Cmdr. Ron Gift of *Monterey,* Cmdr. Bob French of *Franklin,* Lt. Bob Farrington of *Hornet,* and all the other naval airmen of TF 38 would not reach Saipan to enjoy a pleasant rest. Within 24 hours, they would be speeding westward at full speed ahead to launch their biggest carrier strikes against ships since the Battle of the Philippine Sea.

Monday, 8 November, broke gloomy and gray over Manila Bay. Dense, low hanging clouds raced across the harbor, dumping occasional rain squalls that washed the decks of the ships in Convoy One. Meanwhile, blinking lights flicked across the bay like fireflies, as signal men relayed messages from ship to ship to prepare to weigh anchor. On shore, Adm. Akira Shoji, Gen. Tomoyuki Yamashita, and other high officers huddled inside raincoats to watch the ships. Yamashita had visited every vessel in the convoy to urge the troops of the 1st Division to fight honorably in Leyte in the name of the Emperor.

The general's personal presence and fervent appeal to the soldiers on the troopships and destroyer-transports had whipped the men of the Gem Division into a frenzy of patriotism and determination. Every soldier in the convoy, 6,500 of them, promised to fight to the death against the enemy invaders on Leyte.

In the navigation room of flag cruiser *Kumano,* Adm. Mitsui Ijuin sat with other members of his Convoy One staff and with Gen. Tadasu Kotaoka of the 1st Division. The naval officers had charted their 26 hour course and by 0900 hours they would be underway.

"We will not follow the usual convoy route through the Sibiyan Sea and the Masbate Channel," Ijuin told Kotaoka of the 1st Division. "Instead, we will sail further east, along the coasts of Legaspi and Samar Islands. We will then turn into the Camotes Sea and finally into Ormoc Bay. The shoals along this route are dangerous in some areas, but such a route will likely deceive the Americans."

"I understand," General Kotaoka said.

"This dreary weather will be to our advantage," Ijuin continued, "The meterorologists were obviously correct in their forecasts—we will indeed experience several days of foul weather, which will thwart enemy reconnaissance aircraft.

"The Honorable Yamashita has charged my troops with determination," Kotaoka said. "If my troops reach Leyte, they will change the course of battle."

"We will get you there, General," Ijuin said.

Aboard destroyer *Samidare,* Cmdr. Kiyoshi Kikkawa stared from the bridge of his warship and studied the blinking lights from other ships. Kikkawa had been a veteran naval officer for nearly three years of war in the Pacific. He had served during the Guadalcanal and the New Britain campaigns as a combat officer aboard escort destroyers for nearly a year in protecting marus that carried vital raw materials and oil between the East Indies and Japan. By the onset of the Philippine campaign, Kikkawa had been promoted to Lieutenant Commander and given *Samidare*. He had already made several successful runs in the Manila-to-Leyte Express, the 1944 version of the old 1942 Tokyo Express in the Solomons.

Lt. Shegeo Hirayama, *Samidare's* executive officer suddenly stood next to Kikkawa. "We will soon be under way, Commander."

Kikkawa merely nodded.

Hirayama also squinted at the blinking lights, stared up at the low clouds, and then looked at his commander. "This will be the largest convoy to sail into Leyte. The Americans will surely spare no effort to destroy us should they discover us."

"We have excellent anti-aircraft gunners," Kikkawa said, "and we will have heavy air cover. And of course, we will follow an unusual route that will enable us to escape the probing eyes of enemy reconnaissance pilots. But most important, our own scout plane observers have verified the departure of the American carrier fleet that now sails eastward to Saipan. Since the Americans have only a few fighter aircraft in Leyte, they cannot do much damage to us, even if they did find us."

"All that you say should be reassuring," Lieutenant Hirayama said, but still, I am uneasy in such a large flotilla that is such a tempting target."

Kikkawa grinned and tapped his executive officer on the shoulder. "We will reach Ormoc safely, believe me."

On the forecastle of destroyer *Arikaze,* Lt. Kita Madagichi stood stiffly, issuing orders to his deck chiefs. "Tighten all lines and batten down hatches. You will also prepare all guns and alert all look-outs. The sea may be rough and the enemy may conduct submarine or air attacks. We must be prepared."

"Yes, Honorable Commander."

A moment later, Madagichi got a call from the pilot house. "Honorable Commander, we have received the signal from cruiser *Kumano* to get underway."

"Very well," the *Arikaze* commander answered. He then shouted across the deck. "Weigh anchors!"

The rattle of chains soon rasped across Manila Bay as anchors rose upward from *Arikaze* and other ships. Within the next 15 minutes, the vessels pointed their bows and began a slow sail out of Manila Bay. In the lead was picket destroyer *Okinami,* with its radar antenna swirling atop its mast like a horizontal windmill. Behind *Okinami,* side by side, came vanguard destroyers *Hatsuhara* and *Siranuhi,* with flag cruiser *Kumano* right behind the duet. The five marus came next, with the coastal defense ships at their sides. Last to leave the bay were trailing destroyers *Samidare* and *Arikaze,* also with whirling radar antennas atop their masts.

On shore, the VIPs and dozens of sailors watched the 15 ships leave Manila. When they were gone, Yamashita looked at the gloomy clouds and then turned to Admiral Shoji. "The first convoy is underway. Let us pray to our heavenly ancestors that they arrive safely in Leyte."

"I have full confidence in Admiral Ijuin," Shoji said. "He is the best at deceiving the enemy."

"We have taken every precaution, Honorable Yamashita," said Adm. Sato Tomioka, the 1st Transport Fleet chief of staff.

Yamashita nodded.

"I will have the first unit of aircraft off in an hour, Honorable Yamashita," General Tominga now spoke. "They will maintain a cover over the convoy as far as San Bernadino Strait, and then a relief squadron will assume the air cover."

Yamashita stroked his chin. "Kyoji, is it possible to make another attack on Tacloban tomorrow? I realize your airmen were quite successful in the last such attack, but it cannot hurt to make a new assault."

"A wise suggestion," Tominga said. "I should have thought of it myself. I will launch an air strike by the 22nd Air Brigade in Negros. Such an attack will not only cause further damage at Tacloban, but will also act as a diversion for the resupply convoy sailing toward Ormoc Bay."

By 0900 hours, Convoy One had cleared Manila Bay, turned southeast and sailed into the Sibuyan Sea. Destroyer *Okinami* maintained its forward position, with destroyers *Hatsuharu* and *Shiranuhi* in the vanguard positions behind the vanguard destroyer. *Kumano* sailed next in line, and behind the flag cruiser, *Noto, Koshio, Kinka, Koru,* and *Katu Marus* sailed in a hochi checkerboard pattern. To the starboard sailed koshii coastal defense ships #29 and #31, and to port sailed koshii coastal defense ships #33 and #35. Behind these 13 ships, destroyers *Samidare* and *Arikaze* sailed in a slight figure 8 as rear pickets.

Aboard *Koshio Maru,* Lt. Mineoshi Yahiro, CO of Company C, 1st Division's 57th Regiment, stood at the starboard railing and stared at the coastal defense warships to his right. He shifted his feet slightly to compensate for the mild roll of the ship. When Sgt. Kiyoshi Kamiko came next to him, Lieutenant Yahiro turned to face his chief non-com.

"Honorable Yahiro," Kamiko bowed, "all the men are accounted for. They are settled in their assigned quarters and they have checked all equipment. They will be ready when we disembark."

"You have done well," Lieutenant Yahiro said.

"Lieutenant," the sergeant said, "do you believe that we and the other troops of the 1st Division can make a difference?"

"Without a doubt," Yahiro answered.

The convoy sailed on, reaching the southwest coast of Legaspi late in the day. The flotilla steamed during the night and by morning, with dense clouds still overhead, they had cleared the channel between Masbate Island and the island of Samar in the Samar Strait. Thus, with the help of the dreary weather, Ijuin had thus far avoided detection by American scout planes or submarines, and he expected to reach Ormoc Bay sometime this afternoon without interference.

In Manila, Admiral Shoji was ecstatic. Convoy One was approaching its destination without air attacks. He watched confidently as Convoy Three now prepared to leave Manila Bay on this 9 November morning. The 1st Transportation Fleet commander felt pleased with himself. He and chief of staff Tomioka had obviously planned well, taking advantage of foul weather and using an alternate route. Shoji was sure that Convoy Three now leaving Luzon would also reach Leyte without trouble.

The 1st Transportation Fleet Commander had

indeed fooled the Americans. B-24 and Catalina scout planes, although hampered by the heavy overcast, had been flying up and down the Sibiyan Sea between Luzon and Leyte all day on the 8th and into the 9th. They had not detected Ijuin's fleet either visually or on radar, obviously, because the convoy had sailed too far to the east in a different route. The negative radio reports had convinced General Whitehead that new Leyte reinforcement convoys had not left Manila. Further, the general was pleased when four B-25s of the 345th Bomb Group arrived safely this morning at Dulag. He hoped these first bombers would trigger the arrival of more B-25s and A-20s. He would then be well stocked with Mitchells and Havocs when or if the Japanese decided to send another convoy into Ormoc Bay.

Still, Whitehead did not relax his precautionary measures. U.S. recon planes continued their patrols and fighter planes remained on alert. The safeguard paid off. At 1030 hours, 9 November, radar teams picked up blips on their screens. An enemy armada was flying westward, no doubt for a new attack on Tacloban.

"The bastards," Whitehead cursed, "they don't care how bad the weather is. How the hell can they hit anything with these low clouds?"

"I don't know," his aide said.

"Get the fighters out," the general barked.

"Yes sir."

The pilots of the 475th and 49th Fighter

Groups responded quickly: MacDonald, McGuire, Cline, and 21 others from the 475th; Johnson, DeHaven, Bong, and 13 others from the 49th. By 1100 hours, the forty U.S. fighter pilots spotted the sentai of Myrts with their Oscar escorts coming over the Visayan Mountain Range.

Colonel MacDonald cried into his radio. "475th squadrons will take on the fighters, and 49th units will attack the bombers."

"Yes sir," Maj. Jerry Johnson answered.

Both Lt. Ota Tsubo, leading the 16 Myrt dive bombers of the 353rd Sentai, and Lt. Satashi Anabuki, leading 20 Oscars of the 351st Sentai, again failed to seriously damage Tacloban. The 40 Lightnings from the U.S. fighter groups soon decimated the Japanese air formations as they had earlier. The Americans knocked eight bombers and five fighters out of the air and damaged at least six more Japanese planes, with the loss of only one P-38. Only six Myrts reached the Tacloban airfield. In the foul weather, while coming in low under the clouds, a wall of American AA fire struck them and the Japanese lost two bombers. The other Myrts dropped their bombs erratically, failing to damage any of the parked aircraft and punching only one hole in the runway.

The Americans aboard the ships in San Pedro Bay or in the foxholes on Leyte cheered the U.S. air victory. However, on this same morning of 9 November, the U.S. servicemen on the island's east coast might not have been so cheerful if they had been aware of the activities on the other side of the island. By mid-day, Convoy One had turned the corner of northwest Leyte and begun its sail across the upper Camotes Sea toward Ormoc Bay.

Chapter Seven

The U.S. airmen at Tacloban relished their latest air victory, where they had taken another heavy toll against the enemy, with only one P-38 down and no real damage to the Tacloban airfield. In his temporary quarters, Maj. Glen Doolittle of the 345th Bomb Group sat with Capt. Hank Decker, Lt. Ed Dick, and Lt. John Frazier. The four men drank jungle juice highballs of grapefruit juice and ethyl alcohol following the near disaster of the Japanese air units over Tacloban.

Doolittle squinted from the tent and looked at the group's four B-25s of the 498th and 499th Squadrons that had arrived this morning. These Mitchells had been the first land based bombers to reach Leyte. The B-25 bomb bays still carried a pair of 1,000 pound GP bombs and their .50 caliber guns still held loaded ammo belts.

"Jesus, if one of those Nip bombers hit that cluster of Mitchells," Doolittle said, "we could have lost those planes."

Hank Decker craned his neck and looked outside at the low, dark clouds that raced across the sky on this gloomy mid day. "How the hell can those bastards expect to do anything on a day like this?"

"From what I hear," Doolittle scowled, "they even fly through lightning storms or with no visibility at all. They're tenacious sons 'a bitches."

"Do you think they'll be back, Major?" Ed Dick asked.

"I doubt it," Doolittle answered. "They took a good pasting from our P-38 flyboys. I guess they didn't think so many fighters could get off the airstrip. The Nips will probably think about this mauling for a couple of days before they come back."

Capt. Hank Decker tapped his stomach. "It's time for noon chow. They probably haven't got a damn thing except bully beef and dehydrated spuds, but I'm awfully hungry. Maybe it was that long flight from Biak this morning."

"I'm hungry, too," John Frazier said. "I'll go along with you."

At the campsite of the 475th's 431st Squadron, elation reigned among the U.S. fighter pilots. They, along with the pilots from the 49th Group, had downed 22 attacking Japanese planes yesterday and now 13 this morning, with the loss of only two planes of their own. In his tent headquarters, Maj. Tom McGuire sat with three of his pilots.

"Goddamn, Major," Capt. Bob Cline grinned, "we had another field day, almost as good as yesterday. I guess we'll get another whack at them tomorrow."

Capt. Joe Moreing pursed his lips. "I don't think the Nips will be back for a while." He looked at McGuire. "Major, will we be going out ourselves? Maybe on some ground support missions?"

"Maybe," McGuire said as he rose from his chair. "I'm going to take a stroll around the revetment areas before chow. I'd like to see how much damage those Nips did, if any."

"I'll go with you," Bob Cline said.

At the 49th Fighter Group's 7th Squadron operations tent, Maj. Jerry Johnson sat with Capt. Bob DeHaven and Maj. Dick Bong. Among these three U.S. pilots, they had downed 70 planes during their combat careers in the Pacific. DeHaven poured coffee for the two majors, his 7th Squadron commander Johnson and the maverick Bong, who joined any unit that would take him so he could fight in combat.

"Christ, those Japanese never stop coming over Tacloban," DeHaven said.

"We gave them a real show this morning," Johnson said, "but the bitches will probably be back tomorrow."

"Then we'll slaughter them again," Bong grinned. "Pretty soon, they won't have any planes left to knock down."

"Where the hell are they getting all those planes?" Capt. Bob DeHaven shook his head. "Christ, we've been knocking them out of the air ever since we got to Tacloban two weeks ago. The navy guys have been shooting them down since L-day in Leyte, and our AA guys have downed so many of them, the gunners have lost count.''

"They just keep bringing more planes into Luzon,'' Johnson said. "I guess they intend to fight in the Philippines to the end.''

Bong sipped his coffee and then spoke again. "We'll discourage them sooner or later.''

Finally, at the tent quarters of the 110th Tactical Recon Squadron, Capt. Rubel Archuleta sat with Lt. Bob Turner and Lt. Roy Rule.

Turner took a sip of coffee and then shook his head. "Boy, I wish I was up there today in that donnybrook. I would have liked a crack at those Nip fighters.''

"Since we got here,'' Archuleta said, "we've been doing pretty good in our ground support missions at Breakneck Ridge, and we have hit some of that barge traffic at Ormoc. I guess we'll have to settle for that. They don't want these P-40s in dogfights if they can help it.''

"We had a pretty score a few days ago,'' Rule gestured. "I don't give a damn what the Nips have, if you fly these Warhawks right, you can knock down anything.''

"Maybe,'' the captain conceded before he drank more of his coffee. Then he stared beyond his tent at the line of 110th Squadron P-40s. "We were lucky those Nips didn't get many of their planes over the field. They didn't hit a single one of our P-40s.''

"When do you think we'll go out again?'' Lieutenant Turner asked.

"They won't send us out in this weather,'' Archuleta answered. "We'll probably go out tomorrow, either up to Breakneck Ridge or another ground support mission or maybe to Ormoc Bay if our recon planes see any more barges or Sugar Charlies around."

But Turner half sneered. "They're not going to find anything in this kind of weather. The soup must be so thick over the Camotes Sea that recon pilots wouldn't spot a Jap ship if they flew within a hundred yards of it."

"Maybe," Archuleta said.

"Do you think they'll send any more convoys to Ormoc Bay?" Ray Rule asked. "You know—like the one they sent in last week?"

"No," the captain shook his head, "just little stuff like barges and small Sugar Charlies for the time being. They usually take two or three weeks to ready a big convoy fleet." He looked at the low clouds outside. "You know something, Bob, you're right about the soup. I guess this would be a hell of a good day for those Nips to run a supply convoy into Ormoc." Then, Archuleta heaved a sigh and looked at his watch. "Let's get some chow."

"Same old bully beef," Rule grumbled, "but I suppose we can't starve."

"What I wouldn't give for a good PX where I could get myself a nice thick hamburger with plenty of onions on it," Turner said, "or maybe I could get a nice big banana split."

"Dream on," Archuleta grinned.

"Yeh," the lieutenant sighed, rising from his chair and gulping down the last of his coffee.

At 1300 hours, Glen Doolittle got a call from

the operations officer at 5th Air Force ADVON headquarters in Tacloban. "Major, Colonel Hutchinson wants you to take your four Mitchells out this afternoon for a run to Ormoc Bay on the other side of the island. We know the weather is bad, and we know you've had a long flight this morning. But he'd like to see how well the mediums can operate up here during inclement weather."

"Can we expect any shipping targets at Ormoc?" Doolittle asked.

"Not that we know of," the officer answered. "Still, keep your bomb bays full and your machine guns loaded. Fly with full crews. If you run into some barges or Sugar Charlies, you can work them over. We'll send out a couple of squadrons of P-38s with you, one squadron for cover and one squadron with bombs, just in case you get jumped by bandits, or in case you do run into a worthwhile target."

"What time do you want us off?"

"About 1500 hours," the operations officer said. "Is that okay?"

"Yes."

"Okay, we'll tell the tower to look for you."

At 1500 hours, despite the gloomy day, Doolittle and his B-25 airmen took off. Right behind him came 12 P-38s of the 431st Squadron under Maj. Tom McGuire and 11 P-38s of the 7th Squadron under Maj. Jerry Johnson. None of these 5th Air Force airmen had guessed that they would begin one of the most vital air operations of the Leyte war.

At the same 1500 hours, 9 November 1944, the low dense clouds still hung over the Philippines archipelago, including Ormoc Bay. The water had turned glass calm as the day became windless and misty—an excellent time to discharge men and cargo. At 1500 hours, Lt. Mineoshi Yahiro stood along the railing on the main deck of *Koshio Maru,* the big 10,000 ton troopship that carried the entire 1st and 2nd Battalions of the 1st Division's 57th Regiment. The company commander could see the shoreline in the distance, less than two miles away, for the mist had begun to dissipate, despite the clouds overhead.

The men of Yahiro's company had assembled themselves on a patch of open deck on the forward, crammed like sardines in their battle gear, and waiting for their company commander to speak to them. Finally, Yahiro turned, walked to the congested area and addressed his 150 men.

"We have already explained what lies ahead. The Americans have landed on Leyte in force and they are now pressing inland against the brave soldiers of the 35th Army. Our company and the remainder of the 57th Regiment will march to Carigara, where we will join soldiers of the 68th Infantry Brigade and our fellow 1st Division soldiers. For a long time, we have prepared for battle. Now the time has come to use our training and skill. Let us pray to the heavenly spirits to protect and help us in carrying out our duties with fortitude and honor." He paused and then gestured. "When the order comes to disembark, you will leave by squads as we rehearsed during our voyage from Manila.''

The *Koshio Maru* had been moving so slowly to its final destination in the bay that Yahiro did not even know the ship had stopped until the throbbing noise of the engine ceased and the rattling anchor chain plopped into the bay.

Then, Yahiro heard the sound of small engines as a half dozen launch boats putted out from shore toward the big maru. Next he heard the creak of the iron ladder as it dropped slowly along the port side of the hull and ended with a splash on the water's surface. When the yeoman of the first launch boat tied up to the ladder, the harsh voice of Maj. Kusi Imada, the 2nd Battalion commander, rasped across the deck.

"Disembark! Disembark quickly!"

Nippon soldiers, fully clad in combat gear, scrambled down the ladder and leaped into the small craft. The endless parade, like a descending column of ants coming out of a hillside, stopped only long enough for one boat to pull away before the next took its place at the ladder. Yahiro was surprised to see the movement of troops go so swiftly. By 1540 hours, only 20 minutes after the unloading began, his own C Company prepared to disembark. Yahiro cried sharply.

"Down the ladder! Down the ladder swiftly!"

Yahiro then stood at the edge of the gangway and half shoved each jogging soldier that hurried across the deck. He thus accelerated their quick movement down the ladder. Finally, the company commander gave a shove to Sergeant Kamiko before Yahiro stepped on the first rung of the ladder and scanned the deck. Only white clad sailors loitered here now, so he assumed that all of his company had left the ship.

By 1545 hours, his launch boat approached the Ormoc Bay shoreline. But then, suddenly Yahiro heard the whoops of an air raid alarm on shore and he then felt the launch quickly pick up speed and skim hurriedly toward the shore. Soon, ack ack spewed from the destroyers, coastal defense vessels, and the marus themselves. The heavy pom pom of .40 mm AA guns and the booms of 5" guns shuddered the water itself and numbed Yahiro's eardrums. Finally, the C Company commander heard the drone of aircraft beyond the overcast.

Above the clouds, Maj. Glen Doolittle excitedly called his pilots in the four plane B-25 flight. "Did you guys see what's in that bay? Did you see? We'll be going down in single file and you can pick your targets." Doolittle then called the commander of the 7th Squadron. "Redneck Leader," he told Jerry Johnson, "how about coming down with us to hit those AKs and DDs? You can go in first on strafing runs."

"Okay, Major," Johnson answered.

Doolittle next called Tom McGuire of the 431st Fighter Squadron. "Blue Strip Leader, we're going under the overcast to hit targets in the bay. Hang upstairs in case bandits try to stop us."

"Roger," McGuire answered.

Finally, Doolittle called 5th Air Force headquarters in Leyte. "We've run into a horde of

AKs and DDs in Ormoc Bay. They're unloading men and supplies. We'll attack at once, but you've got to send out anything that can help out."

"We'll get the 110th fighter bombers up right away," the OD officer said.

The mist over the bay had all but cleared when the 12 P-38s under Maj. Jerry Johnson zoomed out of the overcast and toward the anchored ships. Despite heavy ack ack fire, the Lightning pilots did not falter. Johnson and his pilots opened with .50 caliber wing fire that laced the superstructures of three ships and ignited deck laden supplies. Luckily, the marus had already disembarked the 57th and 58th Regiment troops. So the Japanese suffered few casualties.

After hitting the marus, the Lightning pilots swooped back and attacked the destroyers in dive bombing attacks and strafing runs. Heavy AA bursts hurt the aim of the Americans, while the same Japanese gunners aboard the warships downed two of the P-38s and damaged a third. Still, the 7th Squadron pilots successfully dropped their 1,000 pound bombs and scored seven hits. One bomb knocked down a mast of a destroyer, a second bomb punched a hole in the forward deck of a warship, and a third bomb ignited fires on another destroyer. Two bombs opened holes in a coastal defense ship that quickly flooded and then settled in Ormoc Bay. Two more bomb hits ruptured the hull of an AK transport.

Now came the B-25s under Glen Doolittle.

However, as the Mitchells emerged from the clouds, the heavy AA fire forced Doolittle to arc his planes away. He led the Mitchells inland and a moment later, the B-25s came over a ridge and once more zoomed into the bay. Doolittle and Lieutenant Dick roared after a transport at masthead height, opening with .50 caliber nose gun fire that silenced the AA gunners on the stern of the ship, but not before Dick suffered a flak hit. Still the lieutenant did a snap roll, skidded slightly to the left and made another attempt to bomb one of the destroyers.

Dick's bombs missed the destroyer and as he droned away, ack ack fire from the warship hit an engine that burst into flames. The lieutenant feathered the prop of the B-25 and started back to Tacloban. However, neither Ed Dick nor any of his crew was ever seen again. They had apparently crashed and perished somewhere in the mountainous Leyte jungles.

Meanwhile, Glen Doolittle glided two bombs into a freighter-transport *Koshio Maru,* damaging the hull with one solid hit, but not opening the hull or starting flooding. Still, the hits destroyed much of the stacked supplies on the deck.

Capt. Hank Decker and Lt. John Frazier, meantime, made their bomb runs on a transport in the face of intense AA fire. One bomb blew away the loading booms on the transport's forward deck, and another 1,000 pounder hit and ignited a deckload of supplies. But as the two planes arced away, a flak burst damaged the stabilizer of Captain Decker's plane and he barely wobbled safely out of the bay. Lieutenant Frazier quickly came alongside to escort Decker back to Tacloban.

Meanwhile, above the clouds, a squadron of the new speedy Jack fighters, 14 Japanese planes, waded into the 12 P-38s of the 431st Squadron under Maj. Tom McGuire, who had hung upstairs to protect the attacking Lightnings and Mitchells. The Americans met the Japanese head on.

"Scramble and attack in pairs," McGuire cried into his radio.

The major and his wingman zoomed into the first V of Jacks. The Japanese evaded the first short bursts of .50 caliber from McGuire's P-38, but the major deftly turned inside one of the Jacks, released more fire, and set the plane afire before the Jack tumbled down through the clouds and crashed in flames inside Ormoc Bay. McGuire then arced in a sharp turn to chase another Jack that came after the major's wingman. Despite the Jack's supposed speed, its 371 MPH velocity was not enough for the P-38 414 MPH velocity. McGuire caught up to the Japanese plane and from a dead stern position he unleashed .50 caliber fire that cut the tail to pieces. The Jack cartwheeled and crashed into the jungle.

Meanwhile, Bob Cline and Joe Moreing ganged up on a Jack that tried to duck into the clouds. The two American pilots shattered the enemy plane with heavy strafing fire before the Jack burst into flames and plunged straight downward, crashed on the shoreline, and exploded in a ball of fire.

During the 15 minute dogfight, the 431st Squadron pilots scored ten definite kills and two probables. However, Lt. Grady Laseter and Lt.

Perry Dahl went down during the dogfight. Dahl had just scored his seventh kill when he destroyed a Japanese plane. But as he arced away, he collided with Lieutenant Laseter's plane and both P-38s fell to earth. Other 431st Squadron pilots saw one parachute open. It was Dahl, who was later rescued by Filippino guerrillas. However Laseter was never seen again and presumed dead.

As the attacking U.S. planes left the area, fires belched and raged aboard many of the ships in the harbor. Luckily, only one coastal defense ship, *Koshii #29,* had been sunk. But, three transports and the freighter-transport had been damaged. Fires had consumed many of the supplies and bombs had destroyed unloading cranes, booms, and davits.

At 1630 hours, Adm. Matsuji Ijuin took stock of his damage. All of the vessels could sail under their own power, but most of them needed repair, or elimination of flooded compartments before they could sail with any kind of speed and maneuverability. The Convoy One commander would have liked to leave the bay but he did not want to get underway with damaged ships because he feared more attacks in the open sea. He had already discharged the 1st Division troops but he could not unload supplies until he repaired unloading equipment on the marus. He called Admiral Shoji in Manila and explained his problem.

"Remain in Ormoc Bay and make repairs during the night," Shoji told the Convoy One commander. "You are not likely to suffer more attacks until tomorrow morning at the earliest. By then, you can get underway, while we can have swarms of fighter aircraft in position to give you cover. You can return to Ormoc Bay and unload supplies when conditions are favorable."

"Yes, Honorable Shoji," Ijuin said.

At 1700 hours, while dense clouds still hung overhead, Lt. Minetoshi Yahiro stood on the Ormoc shoreline and gaped at the bay. In a matter of minutes, the American planes had sent a defense warship to the bottom, while seriously or moderately damaging several other ships, while knocking down about a dozen of the new, renowned Jack fighter planes. Yahiro had never fought the Americans, since he had spent his combat career in China, Southeast Asia, and Manchuria. He had often heard reports about the ferocity and deadliness of American air and sea forces, but he had never before witnessed such attacks personally. He could not believe that a handful of fighters and four bombers could cause so much damage.

Yahiro thanked the heavenly spirits that he had already reached shore and had not suffered death or injury to his soldiers. If he found the American infantry troops at Carigara as aggressive and efficient as these American airmen he would meet a formidable adversary indeed.

However, Yahiro was an officer in charge of men and he could not allow them to see any fear or doubt on his face. He straightened boldly and cried to his men in a calm and authoritative voice. "The engagement is over. Form ranks at once so we may march to our bivouacs."

The soldiers responded quickly to their company commander and they even felt a sense of relief. If Yahiro was not rattled by the air attacks in Ormoc Bay why should they be.

But the show on 9 November was only the beginning. At 1730 hours, eight P-40s of the 110th Recon Squadron under Capt. Rubel Archuleta dipped out of the clouds and skimmed over Ormoc Bay. But AA fire from the big ships was heavy and the captain scowled. Archuleta decided to concentrate on the Ormoc Bay shoreline and warehouses since he could do little against the big ships with a mere eight Warhawks. He called Lt. Robert Turner.

"Rob, take your section over those loaded barges along the shoreline and I'll hit the town with the first section."

"Okay, Rube."

Archuleta zoomed over the town with four planes and the flight dropped eight 500 pounders on a large building, igniting a half dozen huge fires and scattering Japanese service troops. Meanwhile, Lieutenant Turner skimmed over a line of barges where he and his three fellow pilots attacked the small craft with strafing fire and 500 pound bombs. The Americans destroyed at least six of the barges and damaged the others.

At 1740 hours, Archuleta and his pilots disappeared into the clouds, jelled into formation, and droned back to Tacloban.

When reports of the huge convoy in Ormoc Bay reached General Whitehead, he reacted with a

Gen. Walter Krueger, CinC of the U.S. 6th Army, who desperately needed air support in the Leyte battle.

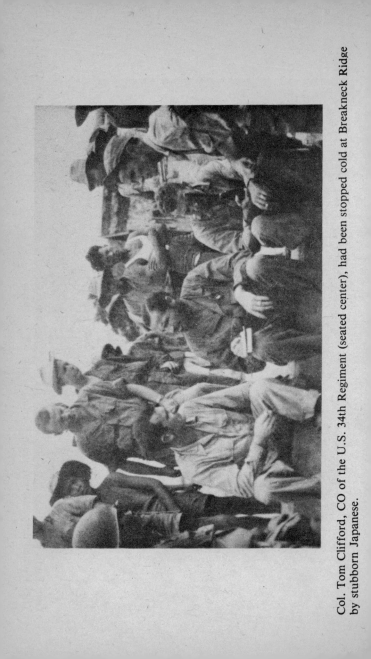

Col. Tom Clifford, CO of the U.S. 34th Regiment (seated center), had been stopped cold at Breakneck Ridge by stubborn Japanese.

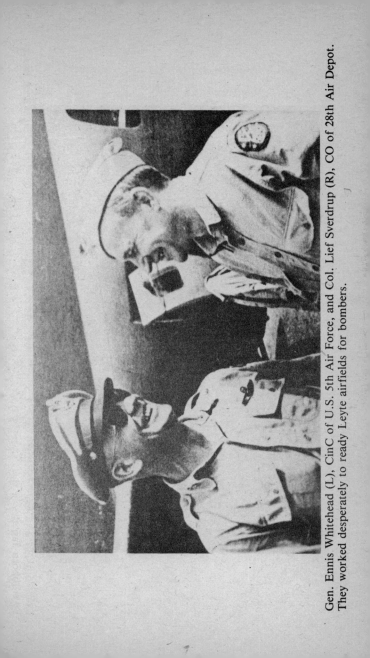

Gen. Ennis Whitehead (L), CinC of U.S. 5th Air Force, and Col. Lief Sverdrup (R), CO of 28th Air Depot. They worked desperately to ready Leyte airfields for bombers.

Maj. Jerry Johnson of the 49th Group's 7th Squadron led his pilots in round after round against Japanese planes over Ormoc Bay.

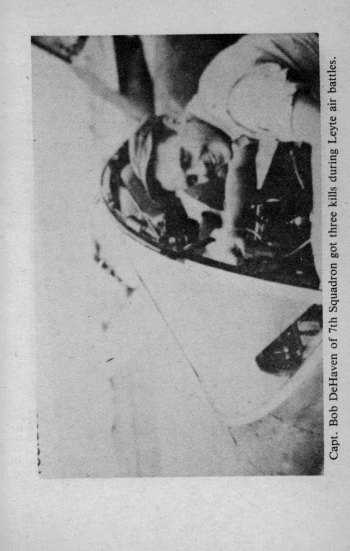

Capt. Bob DeHaven of 7th Squadron got three kills during Leyte air battles.

Col. Charles MacDonald, CO of U.S. 475th Fighter Group, led his pilots in protecting both Tacloban airfield and B-25 bombers at Ormoc Bay.

Maj. Dick Bong, who won CMH after downing eight planes in Ormoc Bay fight.

Maj. John Loisel of 475th's 431st Squadron downed four Japanese planes in air battles over Leyte.

Maj. Tom McGuire of the 475th's 432nd Squadron scored six kills during the ill-fated Japanese TA Operation.

Maj. Glen Doolittle of the 345th Bomb Group's 498th Squadron got the first chance to hit the first Japanese resupply convoy.

Maj. Willian Dunham of the 348th Fighter Group's 460th Squadron did an excellent job of protecting B-25s during attacks on Japanese convoy.

Col. Ed Gavin, CO of the 38th Bomb Group, had trained his men in the use of the skip bomb that became a devastating weapon against Japanese ships.

Maj. Ed Hawes and Lt. Joe Adams of the 38th Group's sank destroyer *Okinami* in vicious skip bomb attack on Convoy One.

Capt. Bob Blair of the 71st Squadron sank the transport *Katu Maru* at Ormoc Bay with a skip bomb attack.

Lt. Jim Fitzsimmons and his crew of *Angry Panther* sank the Japanese coastal defense ship *Koshii 31* but their B-25 was badly shot up. Luckily, they reached Tacloban.

(L to R) Pilots of the 38th Group's 823rd Squadron; Lt. Jim Corn who sank a troop transport, Lt. Zane Corbin who sank cruiser *Kumano,* Capt. John Irick who sank the troopship *Kashio Maru,* and Capt. Dave Bechtel, the group operations officer.

Adm. Fred Sherman, CinC of U.S. Navy's TF 38 carrier group. He had to make a quick reversal back to Leyte in order to attack Japanese Convoy Three.

Navy Secretary Bard (L) presents the Navy Cross to Cmdr. James Mini (R) for his efforts against Japanese Convoy Three. Mrs. Mini (C) looks on.

Cmdr. Ron Gift (L) and Lt. Tom Driess (R) scored their fourth surface ship kill of the Pacific war when they sank Convoy Three's flag destroyer *Hamani*.

Cmdr. Bob Farrington of *USS Horner*'s AG 11 led second element of torpedo bombers against the Japanese flotilla in Sibiyan Sea. He sunk the transport *Kobyo Maru*.

Lt. Cmdr. Bob French (L) of *USS Franklin*'s AG 13 listens to orders in Ready Room with other navy bomber pilots. His unit sank the destroyer *Wakatsuki*.

(L to R) Lt. Art Singer, Lt. Cmdr. Vince Lambert, Lt. Jim Collins. These three torpedo bomber pilots from the *USS Essex*'s AG 4 ganged up on and sank transport *Kamoi Maru*.

Cmdr Dave McCampbell of the *USS Essex* led navy escort planes during attacks on Japanese Convoy Three. He got three quick kills against Japanese fighter plane units.

Lt. Cmdr Ed Anderson of the *USS Ticonderoga* badly damaged a Japanese ship.

Cmdr Tom Jenkins of *Cowpens'* AG 22 sank the transport *Koa Maru.*

Gen. Tomoyuki Yamashita, CinC of the Japanese 14th Army Group for the defense of the Philippines. He initiated the TA Operation to stop the Americans at Leyte.

Gen. Kyoji Tominga, CinC of the Japanese 4th Base Air Force in the Philippines. He promised air cover for the resupply convoys, but his airmen failed.

Gen. Sosuki, CinC of the 35th Army in Leyte. He pleaded desperately for more troops and supplies to push the American troops out of Leyte.

Adm. Akira Shoji of the Japanese 1st Transportation Fleet
carried out the TA Operation to send massive reinforcements
into Leyte.

Lt. Cmdr. Tadashi Nakajima (L) and his aide (R) of his 331st Kokutai. His pilots could not cope with the more aggressive, superior American pilots of 5th Air Force.

(L) Lt. Makase Ibusucki and (R) P/O Arino Kanno of the Japanese 1st Fighter Squadron. Their unit was all but wiped out in dogfights with American airmen.

Capt. Mutohara Okamura commanded the 22nd Air Brigade on Negros Islands. He made a desperate effort to stop American attacks on the resupply convoy, but his airmen failed miserably.

Lt. Satoshi Anabuki, one of Japan's greatest air aces. However, his 351st Sentai air unit was decimated by 5th Air Force fighter pilots.

Gen. Tadasu Kotaoka, CO of the prestigious Japanese 1st Gem Division. He promised to defeat the Americans at Leyte if his troops and supplies got there.

Adm. Muto Matsuyama, commander of Convoy Three, expected
to reach Leyte without difficulty. However, U.S. Navy planes
sank most of his ships in the convoy.

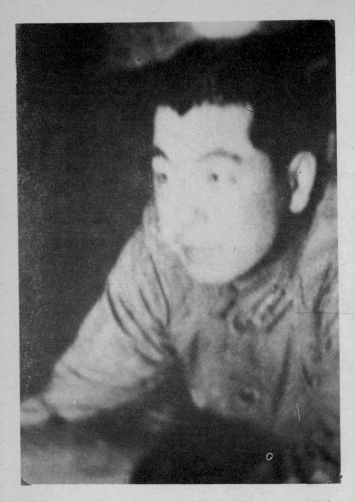
Adm. Matsuji Ijuin, commander of Convoy One, became the victim of the 38th Bomb Group's devastating skip bombing attacks.

Lt. Cmdr. Kiyoshi Kikkawa, skipper of destroyer *Samidare*, was among the few who survived the 38th Bomb Group skip bomb assault.

Cmdr. Arishi Kamiro, skipper of destroyer *Akebono*, found himself in command of Convoy Three after flag ship and fleet staff went down in the flag ship sinking.

The U.S. Tacloban airstrip on Leyte became a frequent target for Japanese bombers.

P-38s burn at Tacloban after Japanese air attack.

Dreaded skip bombers from the 38th Bomb Group drone towards Ormoc Bay.

P-47s of the 348th Fighter Group drone northward to escort B-25s to Leyte.

B-25 of 38th Bomb Group makes a low level skip bomb run on a Japanese transport.

B-25 comes in at masthead height before dropping skip bombs on a Japanese destroyer.

B-25s of the 38th Bomb Group wreck Japanese ships with skip bombs.

A Mitchell pilot of 38th Group strafes a Japanese coastal defense ship. A tandem B-25 will follow to drop its skip bombs into the harassed ship.

U.S. Navy dive bombers score direct hits on a Japanese destroyer in the Sibiyan Sea.

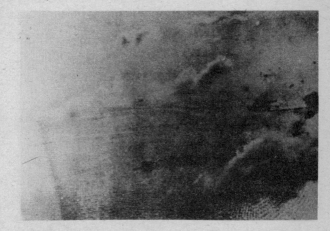

Smoke and fire belch from two Japanese ships after harsh U.S. carrier plane attacks.

The aft of a Japanese transport from Convoy Three catches a torpedo hit from a U.S. Navy Avenger torpedo bomber.

Convoy Three ships sit burning and sinking off the coast of northwest Leyte after a U.S. carrier plane attack.

mixture of shock and irritation. There had been 15 ships in the flotilla, including a quintet of fat cargo-transport vessels. His flyers had only sunk a small warship and damaged several other ships. By this time tomorrow these vessels would be well into the Sibuyan Sea and out of range, and they would come back at an opportune time to discharge cargo as they had discharged troops.

"I want those ships down; all of them down!" Whitehead screamed.

"We don't have anything in Leyte that can put down 14 ships," Colonel Hutchinson of the 308th Bomb Wing said.

"Skip bombs," Whitehead gestured quickly. "We need skip bombing B-25 commerce destroyers and those skip bombing havocs."

"The only skip bombers anywhere near Leyte are the B-25s of the 38th Bomb Group and they're down in Morotai," Hutchinson said.

"I don't care if they're on the moon," Whitehead barked. "Get the 38th Bomb Group to hit that convoy with their skip bombs as quickly as possible. I want their Mitchells off before daylight tomorrow so they can reach that convoy before the enemy ships can get out of range. Get the 18th Fighter Group fighter-bombers up here too. If need be, they can land at Tacloban to refuel before flying back to Sansapor."

"Yes sir," Colonel Hutchinson said.

Chapter Eight

At 1800 hours, 9 November, a message from ADVON 5th Air Force reached the 38th Bomb Group headquarters in Morotai, 675 miles south of Ormoc Bay. While the Sunsetters of the 38th had made bombing runs to Mindanao and even Negros, they had never flown as far as Ormoc Bay. When operations officer Dave Bechtel read the communique, he ogled in astonishment. The captain hurried to the 38th's officers mess to seek out Col. Ed Gavin, the group commander.

"Sir, I'm sorry to interrupt, but I thought you'd want to see this order right away. It's from Colonel Hutchinson in Leyte."

"Hutchinson?" Gavin asked.

"Yes sir," Bechtel said.

Gavin read the message and his eyes widened.

"38th Group will cancel all scheduled FOs and initiate FO 315-X-Al for morning of 30 November 1944 to attack Japanese convoy in Ormoc Bay; To no later than 0700 hours, with ETO at IP at 1130 hours. Group will use all available aircraft and each aircraft will carry 4x500 pound demo five second delay fuse bombs. Each aircraft will also carry a minimum of 7500x50 caliber ammo in forward guns. This order is an OPS priority. Copies have been sent to 348th Fighter Group who will furnish minimum of 20 P-47s as escorts, and to 18th Fighter Group who will furnish minimum of 30 P-38 fighter-bombers to also attack convoy. Signed, Col. Daniel Hutchinson, 308th Bomb Wing, commanding.''

Gavin looked up at Betchel. ''Get a reply off to Leyte right away. Tell them we'll carry out the FO. Then, I want you to crank up a mission plan. I'd like it finished as soon as possible so I can call a briefing at 2000 hours this evening. Be sure squadron line chiefs and ordnance chiefs are at the briefing as well as squadron and flight leaders.''

''Yes sir,'' Captain Bechtel answered.

By 2000 hours, 26 men arrived in the group briefing tent, ad libbing in curiosity. They could not understand why their new group commander had suddenly called this meeting. The officers occasionally looked at the operations officer who loitered on the podium and shuffled through some papers. When Colonel Gavin entered the room, Bechtel stiffened and then cried out.

''Ten-shun!''

The officers rose from their benches and stood erect.

''At ease,'' Gavin gestured. He waited until the

men reseated themselves and quieted down before he leaned over the podium and spoke again. "There's been a change in target for tomorrow. We aren't going to the Halmaheras as planned. The FO has been cancelled in favor of FO 315-4-Al that came down from Leyte only a few hours ago." He paused. "Gentlemen, we're going up to Leyte in the morning to attack a large Japanese convoy in Ormoc Bay."

"Ormoc Bay?" Maj. Ed Maurer cried. "That's got to be at least six hundred fifty miles north of here."

"We'll only be carrying four skip bombs, so we can take extra fuel. We can make the flight and return without difficulty."

The men did not answer, but they looked soberly at their commander. A mixture of anticipation and uneasiness gripped the airmen: Maj. Ed McClean of the 822nd Squadron, Maj. Ed Maurer of the 405th Squadron, Lt. Col. Ed Hawes of the 71st Squadron, Capt. John Irick of the 823rd Squadron, and 22 others. They listened as Colonel Gavin and Captain Bechtel continued.

Gavin explained that information from Leyte said the enemy convoy included at least five transport-freighters, at least a half dozen destroyers, and perhaps as many destroyer escorts. The enemy flotilla had been attacked by four B-25s of the 345th Bomb Group and by fighter bombers of the 49th Fighter Group. The U.S. planes from Leyte had damaged several vessels and perhaps sunk one or two of them. The enemy ships were still in Ormoc Bay, apparently intending to remain throughout the night to make repairs before leaving the bay. The Japanese could probably muster their ships and sail away by late morning tomorrow, probably clearing Ormoc Bay by noon. So, the 38th Bomb Group's B-25s needed to reach target areas as soon as possible.

"Each squadron will mount eight planes," Gavin said. "Maj. Edward McClean will lead the mission, going in first with his 822nd Squadron aircraft. Maj. Edward Maurer will come next with the 405th Squadron, followed by Lt. Col. Hawes in the 71st and Captain Irick with the 823rd. We'll break into squadron units when we reach IP and then break off into pairs, with each duet of aircraft singling out a target. Take off will be at 0700 hours." Gavin then cocked his head at Dave Bechtel. "Captain?"

"Yes sir," the operations officer said. He pulled down a map of the western Pacific on the wall behind him and snapped on a light bulb over the chart. "You'll be flying almost due north over the Celebes Sea, skirting the Talaud Islands along the way. You'll then cross Mindanao Island east of Zamboanga and the eastern part of the Sula Sea. You'll then fly between Cebu and Bohol Islands and then come into Ormoc Bay. If the enemy convoy has left the area by the time you arrive, you'll need to follow the convoy route west and north to catch the Japanese ships somewhere in the northern part of the Camotes Sea. You're likely to find dense clouds over target tomorrow, but that should not bother you since you'll be attacking from minimum altitude. Before you

133

reach IP, you'll get under the clouds and approach targets at three hundred to five hundred feet before making your skip bomb runs."

"Any questions?" Colonel Gavin asked.

"What about interceptors, Colonel?" Major Maurer asked. "Can we expect a lot of bandits?"

Gavin grinned. "I wouldn't be surprised. Make sure your gunners are on alert, and make certain they've got full ammo belts."

"Yes sir."

"We know that AA gunners aboard Japanese ships have been much improved in recent months, so be prepared for accurate flak," Captain Bechtel said.

"We'll have escorts accompanying us from Morotai," Gavin spoke again, "and we might pick up more escorts out of Leyte itself. So we shouldn't have much trouble from Japanese interceptors." He paused and scanned his men. "Anything else?" When no one answered the colonel nodded and then continued.

"Remember, we work in pairs. One pilot strafes, with the other following with a skip bomb attack. Then, you reverse the process."

"We understand, sir," Captain John Irick said.

"Good," Gavin nodded. "Okay get some sleep. We'll have a final briefing at 0600 tomorrow morning, after breakfast. Meanwhile, all line chiefs and ordnance chiefs will make certain that aircraft are loaded and preflighted by at least 0630 hours."

The officers rose from their benches and left the briefing tent in relative silence. For weeks, they had complained about the lack of worthwhile targets, envying the air units now in the Philippines, and wishing that they too saw action on Leyte. They had looked forward to moving north in the near future, but these 38th Group Sunsetters had not expected this sudden, dramatic field order—a long range skip bombing mission on a large Japanese convoy in Ormoc Bay.

At Wama Field, on Noemfoor Island, 220 miles south of Morotai, Maj. William Dunham, CO of the 348th Fighter Group's 460th Squadron, stood in his operations tent with his squadron and flight leaders of his own squadron and of the 461st Squadron. The memo from Leyte had reached Dunham late this afternoon and he was now briefing his men on their escort duties for the Sunsetter B-25s in the morning.

The call for an evening briefing had not surprised these pilots. The group's advance echelon had already left for Leyte aboard an LST and they had arrived in the Philippines yesterday. These pilots assumed that Bill Dunham had called them here for last minute instructions before flying their own P-47s to Leyte in the morning. They were only half right.

The major shuffled through some papers on the podium in front of him before he spoke. "We'll be moving our planes up to Leyte tomorrow as expected. But, there's been a slight change in plans. We'll be conducting a combat mission on our way to Tacloban. 5th Air Force sent us an FO to escort the 38th Bomb Group's B-25s for an attack on shipping in Ormoc Bay."

135

"Ormoc Bay?" Lt. Tom Sheet asked.

Dunham nodded. "There's a huge resupply convoy off the west coast of Leyte. Some of our planes out of Tacloban made a strike on them late this afternoon, but we don't know how much damage they did, if any. General Whitehead apparently feels that the Mitchell skip bombers have the best chance of sinking those Japanese ships, so the 38th will go up in the morning. 5th Air Force expects a sky full of enemy fighters to cover that convoy, so the Mitchells will need good cover of their own."

"What about the fighters already in Tacloban?" Capt. Henry Fleischer asked.

"They'll probably cover the Mitchells, too," Dunham said. "I guess General Whitehead wants as many fighters as possible over Ormoc Bay." He looked at his papers again before he spoke once more. "At any rate, we'll be carrying fully loaded wing guns and a pair of 250 pound GP bombs under our wings. Besides interceptor duty, we may do some dive bombing on those ships ourselves."

"What time are we taking off?" Fleischer asked.

"About 0730 hours," Dunham said. "We'll catch up to the Mitchells over the Celebes Sea. We'll be following a route almost straight north, cross the western arm of Mindanao, the eastern side of the Sula Sea, and then fly between Cebu and Bohol Islands into the Camotes Sea."

"How many of us are going?" Lieutenant Sweet asked.

"Our 460th Squadron plus a flight from the

461st," the major said, "34 planes. I'll lead the 17 P-47s on close cover around the bombers and Captain Fleischer will maintain his 17 P-47s on high cover. As I said, our job is one of escort, but if the opportunity arises, we'll also do some strafing and dive bombing against those ships. We'll go on to Tacloban after the mission since our P-37s can't make a 1200 to 1300 mile round trip without auxiliary fuel tanks."

"Yes sir," Lieutenant Weeks said.

"Okay," the major sighed, "take off is right after breakfast. Meanwhile, we'll notify the line and ordnance chiefs to have all aircraft loaded and revved by 0700 at the latest. Any questions?"

None.

The major gestured. "Dismissed."

The 348th Group pilots in the briefing tent chattered like excited squirrels as they left the meeting. This mission to Ormoc Bay did not frighten them in the least. In fact, excitement reigned because these airmen with their Thunderbolts had always fared well against Japanese fighter planes. The P-47 was stronger, speedier, and more heavily armed than anything the enemy could throw against them. Dunham's warning of a skyful of Japanese fighter planes over Ormoc Bay had only increased their anticipation. After many weeks of slim pickings in western New Guinea and the East Indies, these 348th Group pilots would now get a chance to mix it up in a good donnybrook. Most of the flyers retired early because they wanted to be well rested and refreshed for the flight to Leyte.

At the U.S. airbase in Sansapor, western New Guinea, Maj. William Cowper of the 18th Fighter Group's 70th Squadron also held a meeting with his pilots. Like the combat airmen of the 38th Bomb Group, these men also wondered why their squadron commander had called a briefing on this early evening of 9 November. However, they noticed the aura of excitement on Cowper's face and they guessed that he had important news for them.

"Men," Cowper began with a grin, "we've got a big one for tomorrow; no mission against dead horses. We've received FO 105 from Leyte to supercede any FO we might have had planned for tomorrow. We'll be flying to Ormoc Bay to hit a large Japanese convoy that includes 12 or 15 transport-freighters and warships. The Japanese have been resupplying Leyte with troops and supplies through Ormoc Bay for a couple of weeks, and this convoy is their biggest resupply fleet yet. We'll be carrying 1,000 pound GP bombs under our bellies and we'll also have fully loaded wing guns."

"When do we take off, sir?" Lt. John Haggerty asked.

"The 38th Bomb Group goes off at about 0700 hours with their B-25s and they'll be escorted by the P-48s of the 348th Fighter Group. We'll take of at about 1000 hours and we can expect to be over target area at 1300. It's a pretty long flight, well over 700 miles one way."

"Can we make a round trip that far?" Lt. Ellis Bentley asked.

"We'll go on to Tacloban after the dive bombing runs to refuel before we return to Sansapor," Cowper said.

"Will we need to take on interceptors?" Lieutenant Haggerty asked.

"From what I understand, the fighter groups out of Leyte will engage any possible Japanese escort squadrons. But, if you must, you do have permission to defend yourselves against enemy fighter planes." Cowper looked at his watch and then continued. "Okay, if there's nothing else, the briefing is over. I suggest you get a good night's sleep. We'll have a busy day tomorrow." He turned to an aide. "Captain, make sure that all 14 aircraft are fully loaded and ready for a take off at 1000 hours."

"Yes sir."

As the pilots of the 70th Squadron left their briefing tent, they too chattered excitedly. Like other U.S. fighter pilots in the SWPA, they had also enjoyed excellent success during the past year or more in dogfights with Japanese fighter pilots. The Americans were better trained and their P-38s were superior planes. These U.S. fliers expected good scores if the need arose to engage Japanese pilots in dogfights.

Far to the north, at Tacloban, Col. Charles MacDonald had briefed his P-38 pilots of the 475th Fighter Group. They would take off with 14 planes from the 432nd Squadron at 1000 hours tomorrow to intercept any Japanese planes over Ormoc Bay that attempted to interfere with the B-25 skip bombing attacks. At the 49th Fighter

Group's 7th Squadron briefing tent, Maj. Jerry Johnson briefed 16 pilots. These airmen would take off at 0900 to open the show at Ormoc Bay with fighter-bomber attacks on shipping. Also at Tacloban, Capt. Rubel Archuleta briefed 11 pilots of his 110th Recon Squadron. They would fly off at 0930 hours to dive bomb the convoy with their P-40s, after the P-38 fighter bombers and before the B-25 attacks. The Warhawks would carry fully loaded machine gun belts as well as a pair of 500 pound GP bombs under their wings.

General Whitehead had obviously gone for broke, determined that not a single Japanese ship in that convoy would get away. The 5th Air Force commander had ordered every available plane to attack the large Japanese convoy before the ships could escape from Ormoc Bay or at least the Camotes Sea. He would leave behind at Tacloban only two squadrons of P-38s from the 475th Group's 431st Squadron and the 49th Group's 9th Squadron to protect the field against possible Japanese air attacks. Further, he had instructed Colonel Sverdrup of the 28th Air Depot to keep every available man on duty from dawn to dusk tomorrow to service planes that came in for refueling, so these aircraft could return to their rear echelon bases as soon as possible.

The Japanese, of course, fully expected that American planes would attempt to destroy Convoy One. They were especially worried because Admiral Ijuin had been forced to delay his departure from Ormoc Bay until he could repair the various degrees of damage to his ships. Ijuin needed to make certain that his vessels were in good enough shape to sail as swiftly as possible and to conduct evasive maneuvers against air attacks. He knew the usual fate of ships that tried to run by themselves: they would suffer almost certain demise. The Convoy One commander by the late evening of 9 November again called Admiral Shoji.

"We have been working feverishly on our damaged vessels and we should be ready to sail by mid morning. Unfortunately, damaged booms and davits have deprived us of the chance to unload supplies."

"But the Americans will surely be back. Is it not possible to leave Ormoc Bay by dawn?"

"No, Admiral," Ijuin said. "However, I do not believe the enemy can hurt us badly tomorrow morning, especially if we have the promised air cover at Ormoc Bay. I am certain the enemy has used every one of his available planes this afternoon. Even though they caught us by surprise, they did not do as much damage as we might have expected. They have only fighter aircraft in Leyte, and we shot down the few B-25s they had. All of their bombers are too far to the south to interfere with us."

"Perhaps you are right," the 1st Transportation Fleet CinC said. "I was told by General Tominga that his pilots saw only four bombers at Tacloban and these were apparently the B-25s that your convoy gunners shot down."

"It is my belief, Honorable Shoji, that if indeed

we have the substantial fighter cover as promised, these aircraft can engage further enemy fighter-bombers who try to attack us, and thus leave our convoy relatively free to escape.''

"You can be certain the fighter aircraft will be over your convoy early tomorrow morning. I will also ask General Tominga to launch a new bomber attack against the enemy's Tacloban airfield tomorrow."

"That would be wise," Ijuin said.

Still, Adm. Akira Shoji was not fully confident. He now worried about Convoy Three as well as Convoy One. Matsuyama's flotilla had already left Manila Bay and had come quite far south toward Leyte with 14 vessels that carried one third as many more troops and twice as many tons of supplies as did Convoy One. Thus far, American recon planes had not detected Matsuyama's convoy and Shoji hoped the Americans believed there was no second convoy heading for Leyte.

Shoji's concern for Convoy Two was not as great. This fleet that had left Cagayan, Mindanao, this morning would be sailing north through the Mindanao Sea. They would be within easy range of protective airbases, in Mindanao, Negros, and Cebu. Since potential enemy air attacks would come from Tacloban such American air units were not likely to fly south far enough to find Convoy Two. Still, as a precaution, Shoji asked General Tominga to alert the 4th Air Division in Mindanao to protect Cmdr. Noriteru Yatsui's Convoy Two if such a need arose.

The first Transportation Fleet CinC explained

his other problems to Tominga: the need for Ijuin to wait until at least mid-morning before retiring from Ormoc Bay, the possible detection of Convoy Three that was now entering the Sibuyan Sea, and the need to keep the enemy's Tacloban airfield out of commission.

"It is vital that we have substantial air cover," Shoji said. "Admiral Ijuin also suggests that you make a new bomber attack on the enemy's airfield by first light tomorrow, since any new American air assaults will come from that base."

"I will make arrangements at once," General Tominga promised.

The 4th Base Air Force commander contacted both Cmdr. Tasashi Nakajima of the 331st Kokutai and Captain Mutohara of the 22nd Air Brigade. He ordered both men to prepare every available fighter plane in their units for service in the morning. The 1st Fighter Squadron out of Clark Field would maintain a continual air cover over Convoy Three that was now sailing for Leyte. The 331st Kokutai's 2nd Fighter Squadron as well as the 22nd Air Brigade's 351st and 352nd Sentais would mount all available fighters to protect Admiral Ijuin's Convoy One during retirement from Ormoc Bay.

"The Americans have only a few fighter-bombers to attack the convoy," Tominga told his group commanders. "Had we been prepared for air attacks late this afternoon, the enemy would not even have caused the minor damage they did cause."

"What of the flotilla from Mindanao?"

Captain Okamura asked.

"I have requested that the 4th Air Division use its fighter planes out of Del Monte to protect this convoy. Commander Yatsui's small flotilla will no longer be your concern. We would rather use your fighter sentais for the two larger reinforcement fleets."

"Yes, Honorable Tominga."

"I would also like a new air attack on the enemy's Tacloban airfield in the morning," Tominga continued. "The 22nd Air Brigade will make the first attack at daybreak and the 331st Kokutai will make the second attack a half hour later. Such a tandem assault will certainly cause extensive damage at Tacloban."

"I will not fail," Captain Okamura said.

"Good," the 4th Base Air Force commander answered.

Meanwhile, earlier in the day, at about dusk, a U.S. navy Catalina flying boat spotted Convoy Three just as the flotilla rounded Apapi Point off southern Luzon and headed southeast into the Sibuyan Sea. The sighting shocked the PBY observers. They had heard of the earlier Japanese convoy that 5th Air Force planes had attacked late this afternoon in Ormoc Bay. However, no American had guessed that a second such convoy, equally as large, was also heading for Ormoc Bay.

"Holy Christ," one of the Catalina observers hissed as he ogled at the ships under him, "look at the size of that fleet."

"Goddamn it," the PBY pilot said. "The army hasn't got anywhere near enough planes in Leyte

144

to take on that convoy at Ormoc as well as this new one."

"What are we going to do?"

"Report the findings to the 5th Air Force and the 5th Fleet and let them take it from there."

As soon as the sighting of Convoy Three reached Whitehead in Tacloban and Kinkaid aboard his flagship battleship *New Jersey,* the Americans acted swiftly. Whitehead urged Kinkaid to reverse his carriers and send naval planes after this second convoy heading into the Sibuyan Sea, while the 5th Air Force attacked the convoy in Ormoc Bay.

"Goddamn, Ennis," Kinkaid said, "Sherman is low on supplies."

"Give your dive bombers and torpedo bombers all your available fuel and bombs and we'll give them fighter escort out of Tacloban if you can't finish enough naval fighter cover yourself."

"That might work," Kinkaid said.

"You've got to attack that convoy, Tom," the general insisted. "We can't do it alone."

"Okay," the 5th Fleet commander sighed. He then sent an order to Adm. Fred Sherman of the TF 38 naval carrier force.

Reverse course at once and sail at full ahead to Leyte waters; big enemy convoy sighted off Luzon heading into Sibuyan Sea. You must be in position as soon as possible to launch all available dive and torpedo bombers.

145

The order from Kinkaid jolted Admiral Sherman. His air crews were tired, his planes needed service, and his carriers needed overhauls. Furthermore, his TF 38 fleet was more than 600 miles from Leyte. The TF 38 commander knew as well as anyone that such an enemy convoy with its horde of troops and supplies must not reach Ormoc Bay. Fortunately, all ships had been topped off in fuel. Sherman wallowed in his dilemma for only a few minutes before he issued the order:

"All carriers groups will reverse course at once and proceed at full ahead, 36 knots, to Leyte Gulf. All air groups will prepare as many STB torpedo bombers and SDB dive bombers as possible for air strikes against enemy convoy now in the Sibuyan Sea."

The three fast carrier groups included USS *Essex, Langley, Ticonderoga, Hornet, Cowpens, Monterey, Franklin, Enterprise, San Jacinto* and *Belleau Woods*. Soon, the ten flattops were barrelling to the eastward. They would maintain their fast pace for 30 hours and then start launching planes, as many as 350 of them, against Adm. Muto Matsuyama's Convoy Three.

For two days, November 10th and 11th, great battles of planes against ships and planes against planes would rage over the waters of the central Philippines. Neither side would spare any effort. By dusk of 11 November, the contest would be over. Either the Americans would find themselves in still another stalemated land battle similar to those in the Solomon campaign, or the Japanese would fail in Leyte, a major blow that would herald the loss of the Philippines.

Chapter Nine

Dawn of 10 November 1944 broke clear and dry, a good day for battle: a good morning for a dogfight in the skies over the Philippines, or an assault against the dug-in Japanese on Leyte, or a new bombing attack on Tacloban, or an air attack on surface ships in Ormoc Bay. The Japanese meteorologists had seemingly goofed in their forecast, but, no weatherman on earth could really predict the fickle weather in the SWPA, where thunderclouds often massed or dissipated in minutes.

The day began when the 353rd Bomber Sentai, before daylight at 0500 hours, left Fabrica Drome on Negros Island with 16 Myrt dive bombers under Lt. Tsubo Ota and headed for Leyte.

Tsubo had lost much of his enthusiasm for these bombing raids on Tacloban. On several previous sorties, he had suffered badly against aggressive American fighter pilots in their potent P-38s. However, Captain Okamura had assured the bomber leader that most of the enemy planes in Leyte had probably geared up as fighter bombers to attack Convoy One in Ormoc Bay. Therefore, the American aircraft would be unprepared to repel a formation of Myrts. But Okamura's assurance had not wholly convinced Tsubo, who feared that swarms of Lightnings would still again maul his bomber formation over the Visayan Mountain Range of central Leyte.

The 353rd commander warned his Myrt gunners: "You will remain alert; fully alert for possible interception."

Unfortunately for Tsubo, his fears were justified. By the time the Myrt dive bombers reached the central mountains, the sun had risen over the Leyte hills where vicious land battles had raged for three weeks. The 353rd Sentai had come within 50 miles of Tacloban when U.S. ground observers in Leyte's interior and radar men on the coast again detected the oncoming Japanese bombers.

Gen. Ennis Whitehead, of course, had anticipated enemy air attacks this morning, since the Japanese needed to thwart further U.S. air attacks on Admiral Ijuin's slightly crippled Convoy One. The designated interceptor squadrons had been on stand-by alert since dawn. So two squadrons of P-38s were ready. At 0610 hours, the word reached these fighter units: "Bandits heading for Leyte. All assigned interceptors will scramble at once."

The two squadrons of Lightning pilots, 40 of them, reacted quickly. The airmen of the 475th Fighter Group's 431st Squadron and the 49th Fighter Group's 9th Squadron hurried to their planes. Maj. Tom McGuire led the 431st to attack these reported bombers, while Lt. Col. Bob Morrissey and the 7th Squadron airmen remained on CAP in the event the Japanese had a second formation of bombers heading for Tacloban. By 0630 hours, only 20 minutes after the red alert, the 20 Lightnings of the 475th Group were zooming westward to meet the oncoming Japanese dive bombers.

At 0640 hours, McGuire called Captain Moreing. "Joe, you take the trailing Vs with your flight and I'll take the forward Vs with 1st Flight. Looks like they've got about fifteen or twenty dive bombers, but I don't see any escorts. I can't believe it."

"They'll be goddamn sorry, Tom," Moreing said.

"Okay, scramble!"

"Yes sir," the flight leader answered.

The P-38s then waded into the tight formation of Japanese dive bombers. McGuire caught one of the Myrts with chattering .50 caliber fire that punctured the fuselage before a second burst hit the gas tank and the plane exploded. The fragments and two dead crew members plopped into the mountainous jungles below. Capt. Bob Cline pounced on another trio of Myrts and unleashed heavy .50 caliber fire and several 37mm shells. Cline shattered the cockpit of one Myrt, killing the pilot, before the dive bomber spun dizzily into the jungle hills below. A third 431st pilot sprayed the other two Myrts with machine gun fire. One dive bomber luckily got away, but the second exploded in a ball of fire before the flaming aircraft arced

150

down like a Roman candle and crashed into dense trees.

The Japanese lost still four more dive bombers to McGuire's 1st Flight. One U.S. pilot tore one plane in half with chopping machine gun fire and thumping 37mm shells. Another Myrt lost a tail before plunging into the jungle below. The third lost its right wing, flipped over, and fell like a dead bird. The fourth Japanese dive bomber disintegrated from withering P-38 wing fire that came from three directions.

2nd Flight also enjoyed success. Capt. Joe Moreing dove on a trio of Myrts with blistering machine gun fire that shattered the engine and cowling before the plane plunged into the mountains and exploded. Moreing destroyed a second Myrt with cannon fire, ripping the fuselage to shreds before the plane and its dead crew plunged to earth. Lt. John Harris hit another dive bomber squarely and ignited a ball of fire that whooshed through the fuselage, searing to death the two man crew. The third dive bomber of the three plane V lost a wing and a tail as machine gun and cannon fire battered the aircraft. The plane tumbled downward and crashed into the jungle.

Thus the 475th Group pilots quickly downed eleven of the 16 Myrts in a vicious assault that had not cost the Americans a single plane. The Japanese had made a glaring mistake in sending 16 dive bombers over Leyte without escort,

Lt. Ota Tsubo had no choice but to run off with his five surviving planes. The Japanese luckily droned into a cloud bank to escape further losses from the American Lightnings.

"Okay," Tom McGuire cried into his radio, "let's go home."

"We can finish them, Tom," Joe Moreing complained.

"No," the 431st Squadron commander answered. "The Nips might send more planes over, maybe all day, and we'll need to land and reload to be ready for any more of them."

"Okay," Moreing answered.

By 0700, the 20 431st Squadron pilots had returned to Tacloban. U.S. soldiers on the ground cheered the airmen who had decimated the Japanese bomber formation before the Myrts had even come within sight of the airfield. Col. Charles MacDonald of the 475th Group and Capt. Rube Archuleta of the 110th Recon Squadron felt a sense of relief. Their parked P-38s and P-40s were loaded with bombs in preparation for a new attack on the Japanese ships in Ormoc Bay.

Tom McGuire had acted wisely in not pursuing the remnants of Tsubo's squadron. He had barely landed and taxied off the Tacloban runway when the whining red alert came again, echoing once more across Tacloban and San Pedro Bay. Radar men reported this second Japanese formation of bombers as also numbering between 15 and 20 planes, and again the bombers were coming on without escort, Lt. Col. Bob Morrissey and 15 other P-38 pilots of the 49th Group's 9th Squadron, already on CAP, turned eastward as soon as they got a report on these new interlopers.

"Maybe we ought to send up more planes," an

aide said to General Whitehead.

The 5th Air Force commander shook his head. "No, Morrissey and his boys can take on any unescorted bombers. I want Major McGuire reloaded on the double and standing by in case more Nip planes head for Tacloban. The bastards might send planes over all day. Meanwhile, get the fighter-bombers ready for take-off."

"Yes sir."

By 0715 hours, Lt. Col. Bob Morrissey and his 9th Squadron pilots were zooming westward. Within ten minutes they spotted the enemy planes, 16 Judys of the 3rd Bombing Squadron that had flown out of Mabalacat on Luzon. Lt. Cmdr. Shiuchi Yoshiota had barely reached the Visayan Mountain Range when he saw the P-38s high in the sky.

"Tighten formation, tighten formation!" Yoshiota cried into his radio. "All gunners will remain fully alert."

The Japanese suffered another near massacre. Bob Morrissey stared down at the close Japanese formations before he cried into his radio.

"Okay, attack in pairs; in pairs."

"Yes sir," Lt. William Huiseman answered.

A moment later, Morrissey and his wingman jumped a trio of dive bombers and caught two of the slow moving planes with blistering fire. One Judy exploded from tracer fire and 37mm shells hits. The second dive bomber tried to bank away but two 37mm shells hit, exploded, and blew open the fuselage. The burst ignited the fuel tanks and the plane erupted in a ball of fire. Lt. Cmdr.

Toshiata, leading this first V, luckily escaped the onslaught.

Meanwhile, Capt. Bill Williams caught the lead plane of a second V with 37mm shell hits that shattered the engine. The Judy barrel rolled dizzily, like an albatross gone berserk, before the plane smashed into a hillside jungle of trees.

Within a few minutes, Lt. Cmdr. Yoshiota lost six more Judy bombers. Pairs of P-38s swooped down on the tight Vs from several directions, catching the 3rd Bomber Squadron planes with chattering tracers and thumping shells. The Japanese gunners tried desperately to ward off the attackers, but the single 7.7mm guns could not hurt the sturdily constructed P-38s. While some of the Lightnings had been damaged, none had been lost.

After Yoshiota lost nine of his Judys, he cried into his radio. "We must break off! Break off! We cannot reach the enemy's airfield in the face of so many interceptors."

"Yes, Honorable commander."

The surviving 3rd Bomber Squadron Judys arced away and sped toward the nearest cloud bank to escape further punishment. The 49th Group pilots downed at least one more plane before the remnants of Judys escaped.

"Do we go after them, sir?" Capt. Bill Williams cried into his radio.

"No," Morrissey answered. "We did our job. They didn't get anywhere near the airfield. Like the general said, the Nips may send over more bombers and we've got to land and reload while

154

the 475th pilots take over CAP."

"Yes sir."

Far to the south, a half hour before this second air battle over Leyte, the 38th Bomb Group Mitchells began taking off from Morotai. By 0700 hours, the green light blinked from the control tower and Maj. Ed McClean zoomed down the runway with wingman Lt. Jim Fitzsimmons. A moment later both B-25s were airborne. Then came the six other medium bombers of the 822nd Squadron, including Lt. Ed Polanski and Col. Ed Gavin. As was often customary in U.S. bomber units, the group commander did not necessarily lead the mission. Instead, Major McClean was the mission leader, while Colonel Gavin flew as a flight leader in the 822nd Squadron.

Now, Lt. Col. Ed Hawes of the 71st Squadron roared down the runway with wingman Lt. Joe Adams. Behind Hawes came five more planes, the Mitchells of Capt. Bob Blair, Capt. Harry Sheerer, Lt. Sam Cole, and Lt. Joe Belanger.

Next came the seven B-25s of the group's 405th Squadron. Maj. Ed Maurer, the squadron leader zoomed down the runway with wingman Lt. John Henry. After they arced high, Capt. Bob Nelson and five other 405th Squadron B-25s roared off the apron. Then, they jelled into formation to join the first two squadrons.

Finally, the 823rd Squadron, eight B-25s under Capt. John Irick, zoomed off the airstrip to join the other 22 medium bombers. Behind Irick and his wingman, Capt. Ron Bauers, came Capt. Luke Lupardas and his wingman and then Lt. Jim

Corban and his wingman. Last to take off was Capt. Zane Corbin and his wingman. When the 30 Sunsetter bombers jelled into formation above Morotai Island, they soon disappeared into the northern sky.

Operations officer Dave Bechtel turned to his aide. "I hope to hell they make it okay."

"They'll be okay," Lt. Hugh O'Brien answered. "Our guys have been skip bombing for a long time and the colonel has them as sharp as razors. They'll get some good scores."

Bechtel frowned. "Six hundred seventy-five miles is a long way. They could start running into interceptors even before they reach the Mindanao coast. Those new Jack fighters the Nips have are goddamn good."

"So are the B-47s and those 348th Group pilots," O'Brien grinned.

Bechtel nodded.

An hour earlier, at Noemfoor Island, Maj. Bill "Dinghy" Dunham had left Wama Field with 34 Thunderbolts of the 348 Group's 460th and 461st Squadrons. By 0700, the P-47s had passed Morotai, turned swiftly northwest, and droned towards the Celebes Sea. By 0800, when the Thunderbolts passed Sangine Island, Dunham knew he would soon rendezvous with the 38th Bomb Group.

At 0830 hours, in the lead B-25 of the 38th Group, Maj. Ed McClean looked at his watch, frowned, and then called his turrent gunner. "Sergeant, any sign of those escorts?"

"No sir," the gunner answered.

"As soon as you see them, let me know."

"Yes sir."

Aboard Lt. Ed Polanski's plane, co-pilot Carl Bliek of Roundel, Wisconsin continually stared from the starboard window, hoping to see the P-47 escorts: Polanski grinned at the young lieutenant. "Don't worry, they'll make the rendezvous. We're still early."

The co-pilot nodded.

"They've never failed yet," Polanski said. He then picked up his radio and called turret gunner Fred Hellman of Chicago. "Sergeant, any sign of escorts?"

"No sir."

"Stay alert. Report as soon as you see them."

"Yes sir."

In the fuselage, engineer-gunner John Gaffney of Upper Darby, Pennsylvania, toyed with his equipment. Occasionally, the sergeant squinted from one of the waist windows, but he still saw nothing except his fellow B-25s. Gaffney grew more uneasy with each passing moment because he dreaded this long three hour flight over enemy territory. In the tail, gunner Wilfred Gable of Los Angeles squinted at the diamonds of B-25s behind him. The corporal also feared this long flight to Leyte. He did not doubt that Polanski would make a good skip bomb run, but he worried about interceptors and heavy AA fire. Finally, in his small compartment, navigator Bill Crutchfield of Memphis, Tennessee, looked at his chart and then his compass. They were now deep over the expansive Celebes Sea. Lieutenant Crutchfield hoped the P-47s would come soon, before his B-25 got jumped by bandits out of Mindanao.

In A/C *Angry Panther,* Lt. Jim Fitzsimmons looked at his chart to find the small isle he had seen off to his right. He could not locate the landmark on the map and he scowled. "Goddamn it, how come they don't have that island listed."

"I guess they missed it," co-pilot Don Raymond answered.

"They're supposed to be good; not miss a thing."

"Nobody's perfect," Raymond grinned.

Fitzsimmons called his navigator, Joe Gulley, "Lieutenant, do you have an idea where we are?"

"About fifty miles northwest of Sangine Island. We're nearing Checkpoint One for rendezvous with the fighters."

"Okay," Fitzsimmons answered. He then called his gunners. "Do any of you see anything? Any sign of our escort? Or even bandits?"

"No sir," waist gunner Bob Tate answered.

"Not a thing, sir," turret gunner Roger Cloutier answered.

"Nothing yet, sir," tail gunner Harry Martin answered.

"Call me if you see anything."

"Yes sir," Sgt. Bob Tate said.

The gunners aboard *Angry Panther* felt the same anxieties as crews on other Sunsetter B-25s. Radio gunner Tate continually peered out of a waist window, hoping to see the P-47s. Engineer-gunner Roger Cloutier scanned the empty blue skies from his position, wondering about interceptors. Tail-gunner Harry Martin held his gun triggers so tightly, the back of his hands had turned blue. He felt perspiration dampen his body, even at this cool 8,000 feet altitude.

In the 405th Squadron, Maj. Ed Maurer shuttled his glance between the instrument panel and the clear skies about him. He squinted through the windshield and faintly saw to his right a small isle that appeared deserted. However, the tiny island might have a Japanese radar station or coast watcher post. The enemy might have seen these B-25s and the Japanese could send out fighters from Mindanao. The major called Capt. Bob Blair, who led the second element of 405th Squadron planes.

"Captain, tighten formation and make sure all gunners are alert."

"We haven't seen a sign of bandits, Major," Blair answered.

"We might," the major said.

"Okay, I'll pull our planes in close."

Behind the 405th Squadron, Lt. Col. Ed Hawes in the lead 71st Squadron plane squinted from his window and stared at the hanging B-25 of his wingman, Lt. Joe Adams. Then he frowned. Adams was drifting away. Hawes picked up his radio. "Lieutenant, you're too far off. Tighten up. We're getting close to Mindanao and the Nips could send out fighters from Zamboanga."

"Yes sir," Adam answered.

Hawes then looked at his chart and called the other pilots of his squadron. "We're at Checkpoint One for rendezvous with escorts. All personnel stay alert. Report as soon as you see those Thunderbolts.''

"Or see bandits,'' Capt. Harry Sheerer answered dryly.

"Yeh, or bandits,'' Hawes said. "Anyway, keep alert, and make sure all gunners are on the ready.''

"Yes sir.'' Now it was Lt. Sam Cole who answered.

To the rear, in the 823rd Squadron, Capt. John Irick looked at his instrument panel. Altitude 8,000; speed 210 knots. They were flying at established height and speed. He squinted at the bomb release button and he wondered if he would score with the skip bombs today. He lightly touched the trigger button of his forward firing guns. Irick had never ceased to marvel at the deadly commerce destroyer, this B-25 with its horrendous .50 caliber guns protruding from the nose and forward fuselage and the pairs of deadly low level skip bombs in the bomb bays. Rarely had Japanese surface ships escaped destruction or damage from these modified Mitchells. The 823rd Squadron commander knew that Japanese ship commanders dreaded the commerce destroyer more than any other American plane in the U.S. arsenal.

Since the Battle of the Bismarck Sea, 1½ years ago, Japanese shipping had suffered badly from commerce destroyers. Now, with a big convoy reported in Ormoc Bay, Capt. John Irick hoped the 38th Bomb Group's skip bombing Mitchells could conduct a replay of that stunning Bismarck

Sea victory. The 823rd Squadron commander looked at the emptiness ahead of him and then called his pilots.

"Keep formation tight; keep it tight. Make sure all gunners are on the ready. Nip planes could come out of the north."

"We hear you, Captain," Lt. Jim Corn answered.

"We'll be alert," Lt. Zane Corbin said.

"We'll keep our eyes open," Capt. Luke Lupardas said.

Since the 823rd would go in last, Irick and his fellow pilots felt apprehension. They wondered if the whole show might not be over by the time they made their runs. Lt. Jim Corn had enjoyed only slim pickings in recent months, mostly small Sugar Charlies and even smaller barges. He hoped to get a nice fat transport on this mission. Lt. Zane Corbin had not seen anything larger than a 500 tonner since he came into combat a year ago and he too daydreamed, envisioning a big warship going under after telling skip bomb hits. Capt. Luke Lupardus had destroyed nothing but barges over the past several months and he too yearned for a plump target, especially after flying nearly 700 miles.

At 0930 hours, tail gunner Ira Nelson on Lt. Jim Corn's trailing B-25 in the 38th Bomb Group formation, abruptly stiffened in his small compartment. He saw dots in the distance behind him, a formation of planes. However, he could not tell if they were friend or foe. For nearly a full minute he ogled at the oncoming shapes and then a grin creased his boyish face. He called Lieutenant Corn.

"Sir, escorts coming up. Escorts."

Corn craned his neck to look, but he could not yet see the P-47s from his cabin window. A moment later, however, Corn's turret gunner also cried into his intercom: "Sir, P-47s coming on fast."

Before Corn answered, the VF channel came alive. "This is Sandy Leader, Sandy Leader," the voice of Maj. Bill Dunham came over the radio. "We'll be assuming a high and ring position, with two scouts out front."

"We read you, Sandy," Maj. Ed McClean answered. "And I must say, we're goddamn glad to see you."

"We're right on time, Major, on time," Dunham said. "How far to target?"

"About an hour and a half."

"We'll be with you all the way," the 460th Squadron commander answered.

The crews aboard the Sunsetter bombers stared in relief as the P-47s swarmed about their Mitchells. 16 Thunderbolts quickly hung around the bombers like a protective chain, while 16 more climbed upstairs to hang over the Mitchells like an umbrella. Two Thunderbolts zoomed forward to assume picket positions. These van P-47 pilots would report any sign of enemy planes.

At 1000 hours, the 30 skip bombers and their 34 P-47 escorts reached Mindanao Island and Col. Ed Gavin looked at his watch. They were an hour or more from IP. The 38th Group commander licked his lips. He had worked hard to help airmen in the skip bombing technique and he hoped they could score big today, not only to hurt the enemy but to boost the morale of his crews. Then, he got a call from Maj. Ed McClean.

"We're right on schedule, sir. We'll break into squadrons within two minutes of IP and then in pairs for runs over target."

"Good," Gavin answered McClean.

In Ormoc Bay, Admiral Matsuji Ijuin had become impatient as the morning sun rose higher in the east. He did not like this delay in getting Convoy One under way, and he liked even less the cloudless day, an unexpected development that had not been predicted by the meteorologists. Ijuin left the deck of flag cruiser *Kumano* and walked to the communications room. "Have ship commanders completed repairs?" he asked the radio officer.

"Yes, Honorable Ijuin," the officer answered. "They are now getting ready to weigh anchor."

"Good, good," Ijuin nodded. "You will signal all commanders to assume their assigned positions in the bay. Destroyer *Okinami* will take the picket position and destroyers *Hatsuhara* and *Shiranuhi* will take post positions. The koshii warships will assume flank positions for the marus, and destroyers *Samaidare* and *Arikaze* will take the rear picket formation."

"Yes, Honorable Ijuin," the radio officer said.

Soon, the clank of anchors echoed across Ormoc Bay, while signal flags rose and fluttered on the more than a dozen ships. Firemen worked up steam, helmsmen set courses, and work crews battened down hatches. The soldiers of the 1st Division watched glumly from the shoreline. While they themselves had safely disembarked, their supplies and guns had not come ashore.

Gen. Tadashu Kotaoka, the Gem Division commander, had reluctantly agreed with Admiral Ijuin's reasoning. Convoy One must retire from the bay while the ships still faced danger from enemy air attacks. They could only return to unload supplies when conditions became favorable. Kotaoka knew that two formations of bombers had gone out this morning to assail Tacloban. If the bombers succeeded in knocking out the U.S. airfield, perhaps Ijuin could return as early as this afternoon. The 1st Division commander, of course, did not know that both 4th Base Air Force bomber units had been shattered earlier this morning by U.S. P-38s.

At 1020 hours, the sky over Ormoc Bay came alive with aircraft. Sailors and soldiers looked up at the swarm of Zeros from the 331st Kokutai's 2nd Squadron that had arrived to protect the retirement of Convoy One. The Japanese on the ground and aboard ships waved and cheered. Aboard *Kumano,* Admiral Ijuin stared from his radio room and grinned.

"The air cover is here."

A moment later, a call reached the flag cruiser's radio room from Lt. Muto Yokoyama, the commander of the 2nd Squadron. "We have 24 fighters aloft and we will accompany you as far as

Masbate Island. Then, a relief squadron will assume cover.''

"Excellent," Admiral Ijuin answered.

But only moments away were 16 Lightnings of the 49th Fighter Group's 7th Squadron under Maj. Jerry Johnson, and 14 Warhawks of the 110th Recon Squadron under Capt. Rube Archuleta. These U.S. fighter-bombers would attempt a new assault on Convoy One, while the Zero fighters tried to stop them in this next round of this turbulent 10 November 1944 day.

Chapter Ten

Just as the ships of Convoy One moved into assigned positions to leave Ormoc Bay, air raid sirens blared out of Ormoc town and echoed across the bay. Maj. Jerry Johnson was coming in with the 16 Lightning fighter-bombers of the U.S. 7th Squadron. Capt. Rube Archuleta was right behind the 7th with twelve P-40s of his own 110th Recon Squadron. Japanese AA gunners on the shoreline and within the town quickly manned gun pits, while Nippon sailors aboard the vessels in the harbor hurried to their own AA positions. Admiral Ijuin darted out of the radio room to the top deck of cruiser *Kumano* and squinted to the east, but he did not yet see any planes. However, he turned to an aide.

"You will notify the commander of our aircraft that covers us to attack these interlopers at once."

"Yes, Honorable Ijuin."

However, Lt. Muto Yokoyama, the 2nd Fighter Squadron leader, had already received an alert from the Japanese radar men at Ormoc. "We are on the way," Yokoyama told Kumano's radio man. "I would suggest that you not delay your departure."

"I will relay your suggestion to Admiral Ijuin," the radio man said.

Jerry Johnson saw the Zeros coming toward him and the major cried into his radio. "Second element of 7th Squadron and the 110th Squadron will carry out their fighter bomber attacks on enemy ships. First element of the 7th Squadron will take on interceptors."

"There's couple dozen planes coming at us, Jerry," Capt. Bob DeHaven said. "Are you sure you can handle them with eight P-38s?"

"We'll try," Johnson answered. "If we can't do it, you'll need to come up and join us."

"Okay," DeHaven said.

A moment later, Johnson and seven fellow pilots zoomed high in the sky, while Capt. Bob DeHaven led the other eight Lightnings low to attack the convoy. Right behind DeHaven, Capt. Rube Archuleta followed with his twelve P-40 fighter-bombers.

"Attack in pairs, in pairs," DeHaven cried into his radio.

"Okay," Archuleta answered.

However, the American fighter-bombers ran into a wall of shipboard AA fire, heavy and accurate. One flak burst caught a P-38 and blew open its belly before the Lightning plopped into the bay, killing the pilot. Another mass of flak enveloped a second P-38, chopping off the forked tail, one wing, and parts of the fuselage before the fragments splashed into the water. One of the

110th Squadron's P-40s caught a flak burst that ignited the bombs under the wing and the Warhawk blew apart in the subsequent explosion.

However, the American fighter-bombers did hit Convoy One. Four P-38s escaped the heavy flak to release their GP 500 pounders against destroyer *Okanami*. The first two pilots scored hits on the stern and destroyed the torpedo tubes. Another P-38 got two hits on the superstructure, smashing a storage locker, igniting the pilot house, and killing the helmsman. The destroyer steamed about erratically, while smoke and fire raged over the main deck. Then, Major DeHaven and his wingman came down and attacked the stricken destroyer with four 500 pound bombs. Two exploded squarely on the water line, opening holes. As sea water poured into the ship, the destroyer listed to port and slowed to a crawl.

However, *Okinami's* crew worked furiously and effectively sealed flooding and doused shipboard fires. Repair crews got the ship set on manual steering since the pilot house had been destroyed. Thus, despite the list, the Japanese destroyer zigzagged away and avoided further damage.

Meanwhile, Capt. Rube Archuleta dove on destroyer *Hatsuharu* with a quartet of P-40s that also met a barrage of AA fire. A burst of flak ripped open the fuselage of one P-40, but the other three dropped a trio of 500 pounders. However, because of heavy flak and a Japanese smoke screen, only one of the three bombs hit the destroyer to wreck the plotting room and a 5″ turret gun.

"We'll circle back," Archuleta told his pilots. "Next time, we'll open with strafing fire before we release bombs."

However, Lt. Roy Rule in the second element of the 110th Squadron gave the captain a shocking answer. "Rube, they've got a real donnybrook upstairs. The Nips have come in with another full squadron of fighters and the P-38s can't handle them all. They need help."

"We're supposed to be hitting these ships," Archuleta said.

Suddenly, two Oscars zoomed from upstairs and unleashed 7.7mm wing fire that tattooed Archuleta's plane, but did not seriously damage the P-40. Then, the captain ogled in awe when he saw a P-38 chasing another Oscar. A moment later, Archuleta heard a new chatter of machine guns before he saw an Oscar explode. The captain's wingman, Lt. Joe Regan, had caught the Japanese fighter plane and blew it apart before the enemy pilot could hit the 110th Recon Squadron commander.

Archuleta now yelled into his radio. "Okay, we've had enough. Those goddamn Nip interceptors are all over the place. Jettison bombs and let's get them."

"Yes sir," Lt. Bob Turner answered.

Both the P-38s and P-40s had only damaged two destroyers of Convoy One before they were forced to break off their attacks on the Japanese ships to engage a horde of enemy fighters. Further, the abbreviated attack had cost two P-38s and one P-40

On cruiser *Kumano,* Adm. Matsuji Ijuin glee-fully witnessed the break off by the American fighter-bombers. "Our fighter aircraft stopped the Yankee dogs. Notify all commanders to continue retirement course, while our brave pilots destroy these interlopers."

"I regret to say, Admiral, that our vessels are now scattered all over the bay," the aide answered. "They took evasive action as soon as the enemy began its dive bombing attack. We will need to reform."

"All right," Ijuin scowled. Then he gestured. "But tell them to reform as quickly as possible."

"Yes, Admiral."

Maj. Jerry Johnson had indeed found himself badly harassed. Not only had he engaged the 16 Zeros of Lieutenant Yokoyama's 2nd Fighter Squadron, but 16 Oscars had arrived from Negros to join the 2nd Squadron. When the Japanese learned that their bomber units had failed to reach the Tacloban airfield, Capt. Mutohara Okamura had acted at once. He rightly guessed that the abortive bombing missions would enable the Americans to launch fighter-bomber attacks on Convoy One. So the captain had wisely sent off 16 Oscars to join the 16 Zeros over the convoy, hoping they'd be over Ormoc Bay before the American fighter-bombers arrived. Okamura's decision paid off. Only moments after the P-38s and P-40s began their dive bombing attacks, these Japanese army fighter planes arrived in the battle zone to aid the navy fighter planes.

Lt. Satashi Anabuki and his Oscar pilots of the

351st Sentai had wasted no time in attacking the P-48 and P-40 fighter-bombers, while Lieutentant Yokoyama kept Maj. Jerry Johnson and his seven fellow topside pilots at bay. A two to one advantage on the part of the Japanese had compensated for the speedier P-38 and their better trained airmen.

But now, the odds had changed: 25 P-38s and P-40s against 30 Zeros and Oscars (both sides had already lost planes). Even the P-40, somewhat inferior to the Zero and Oscar, became a formidable opponent when piloted by cagey, experienced pilots, such as the airmen of the 110th Recon Squadron. The 4th Base Air Force pilots again faced such adversaries as the potent Jerry Johnson, the intrepid Bob DeHaven, the spunky Elliot Dent, the incomparable Dick Bong, the bulldog Rube Archuleta, the plucky Bob Turner, and the audacious Roy Rule. While Convoy One had escaped with minimum damage, the Japanese air squadron would enjoy no such luck.

Jerry Johnson and his wingman waded into a trio of Zeros with chattering machine gun fire and whooshing 37mm shells. The two pilots knocked one Zero out of the sky when they chopped apart the plane and the fragments dropped like heavy chunks of confetti. They badly damaged a second plane that arced away with streaming smoke. The Zero pilot would never get back to Luzon, but would need to ditch because of his damaged engine.

Capt. Bob DeHaven and his wingman pounced on another trio of Japanese Zeros. DeHaven got the lead plane when he shattered the cockpit with a direct 37mm shell hit that killed the pilot. The plane tumbled downward and crashed into the sea. The captain's wingman also got a Zero when he shot away the tail of a Japanese plane and the aircraft tipped over before flitting into the sea. However, the Japanese pilot successfully bailed out, and a launch boat out of Ormoc plucked him from the sea.

Meanwhile, Maj. Dick Bong and his wingman waded into a trio of Oscars from the 351st Sentai, that had arrived from Negros. Bong, as accurate and cagey as ever, maneuvered his P-38 deftly into position to knock down all three Japanese planes before any of them escaped. He caught the lead Oscar with ripping machine gun bursts that smashed the cockpit and killed the pilot. He then made a quick turn and pursued the second Oscar which tried to arc away. Bong hit the enemy plane with chattering tracer fire. The aircraft plunged downward and splashed into the sea.

Bong then circled high, made a sharp turn, and zoomed after the third Oscar in this three plane V. The Japanese plane moved swiftly east, but the major quickly caught up with the aircraft with his speedier Lightning. He unleashed chattering wing fire that ripped into the fuselage of his victim before the Japanese pilot could maneuver away. Then, the American air ace sent a pair of 37mm shells into the plane and the Oscar exploded in mid air. Bong then veered his plane up and away to escape flying debris from the bursting Oscar.

Capt. Elliot Dent also scored when he and his

wingman chased a pair of Oscars that were zooming at low altitude over the bay. The Japanese pilots apparently hoped that the AA gunners of Convoy One would knock down or at least chase off the American pursuers. But, no luck. Dent caught one of the Oscars with ripping .50 caliber machine gun fire and the Oscar plopped into the water, skidding across the surface and then sinking in the bay. Dent's wingman finished off the second Oscar with an exploding 37mm shell that tore off the tail before the Japanese plane cartwheeled into the sea with a resounding splash.

The pilots of the 110th Recon Squadron enjoyed equal success. Since much of the air action prevailed at low altitude, where Warhawks matched the Zeros and Oscars, the P-40 pilots scored well.

Captain Archuleta and Lieutenant Regan, after their first encounter with Japanese fighters, now pursued a trio of Oscars at almost deck level across the bay. Archuleta unleashed a deflection burst from 40 degrees, but missed. However, Regan forced the Japanese pilot to bank away and Archuleta found himself dead astern of the Oscar. The captain fired a short burst that shattered the cockpit. The Japanese plane flipped on its back and plunged into the water. The 110th Recon Squadron commander then pursued a second Oscar with his wingman. Now, as Regan got behind the plane, the Japanese pilot made a complete 360 degree turn only to find himself in front of Archuleta, who fired his wing gun and damaged the enemy aircraft. Unfortunately, the captain's guns jammed, so he could not get in another burst. So the damaged Oscar got away.

Capt. Roy Rule and wingman Bob Turner, who had attacked a Japanese destroyer earlier, also scored in this dogfight. The two American pilots came out of an overcast and spotted two Japanese Oscars, one climbing behind them and the second flying under them. The two Americans went after the low Oscar with blistering tracer fire. Turner missed, but Rule chopped apart the fuselage of the Japanese fighter plane that smoked badly before plopping into the bay. The U.S. pilots then chased the second Oscar and caught the plane above the Ormoc jungles. Rule and Turner opened with chattering wing fire and chopped off the Oscar's left wing before the Japanese fighter plane upended and crashed into the jungle.

Other P-38 and P-40 pilots also scored. In fact, during the 15 minute donnybrook, the Americans downed nine Oscars from Lieutenant Anabuki's 351st Sentai and seven Zeros from Lieutenant Yokoyama's 2nd Fighter Squadron. The American had damaged at least six more of the Japanese fighter planes. In turn, the Japanese pilots had only downed three planes, one P-40 and two P-38s. The Americans thus lost six planes, counting the three downed by Convoy One AA gunners.

The adept Satashi Anabuki, the long time combat veteran with 40 kills in the Pacific, had scored two of the kills for the Japanese. He caught a P-40 when he dove from above and opened on the unsuspecting American pilot with chattering 7.7 wing fire and 20mm cannon fire. The Warhawk exploded, killing the pilot, before the P-40 splashed into Ormoc Bay. Anabuki got his second score when he deftly maneuvered away from a tailing P-38 and then came down on a surprised Lightning pilot. The 351st Sentai commander shattered the right wing of the P-38 with exploding 20mm shells and the Lightning fell on its side and tumbled into the sea.

Lieutenant Yokoyama got the third 4th Base Air Force kill when he caught a P-38 that arced away after downing an Oscar. The 2nd Fighter Squadron commander caught the Lightning with an exploding 20mm shell burst in the cockpit that killed the pilot. The American fighter plane crashed into the sea.

The vicious brawl had left both sides spent, with almost all ammunition and cannon shells exhausted.

"Okay, back to Tacloban," Maj. Jerry Johnson cried into his radio. "We can't do anything more here."

"What about all those ships?" Capt. Elliot Dent asked.

"Leave them for the B-25s."

"We read you, Major," Capt. Rube Archuleta said.

As the American planes arced away to fly eastward, Lt. Satashi Anabuki also cried into his radio. "We are spent, and we must return to base. The 351st Sentai will fly to Bacolod Field and the Kokutai aircraft will return to Mabalacat."

"But what of the convoy?" Lieutenant Yokoyama asked.

"They should be safe now, for we have stopped the American fighter-bombers that attacked the vessels. In any event, a new squadron of aircraft will soon arrive to maintain air cover over the marus and warships."

"Yes, Lieutenant," Yokoyama answered.

On the surface of Ormoc Bay, Adm. Matsuji Ijuin watched the adversaries fly off, the Americans to the east and the Japanese to the west and northwest. He felt quite satisfied. With the help of these Japanese fighter pilots, he had suffered only minor damage, and he expected no further problems from the American air forces. He would need to leave behind only the listing destroyer that could hug the coastline and hide in some of the caves to continue to journey during the night. The second destroyer, *Hatsuhara,* had been only slightly damaged and she could easily keep up with the remainder of Convoy One.

The Convoy One commander called Adm. Akira Shoji in Manila. "Honorable Shoji, the Americans have attacked our vessels with aircraft, but they did little damage, except for destroyer *Okinami.* However, the warship is afloat and under its own power. We can thank the anti-aircraft gunners and the brave fighter pilots who effectively thwarted the American attack."

"Good," Shoji answered. "I have been informed that Commander Yatsui's small convoy left Cagayan on the north coast of Mindanao early last evening instead of waiting until this morning.

He is therefore well into the Camotes Sea by this time and he should arrive at Baybay sometime early this afternoon. Also, Admiral Matsayuma's larger convoy is now sailing along the coast of Masbate Island and he should arrive on the west coast of Leyte sometime tomorrow, probably at dusk."

"I see."

"You will sail northwest into the Camotes Sea. If there is no further interference from the Americans, you can return to Ormoc late this afternoon and perhaps unload your supplies this evening. Reconnaissance aircraft are flying to Tacloban to make certain that no more enemy aircraft come to Ormoc Bay."

"But the booms and davits on the transport-cargo marus are badly damaged, although we have been working on them since yesterday. They are not yet repaired."

"Can they be repaired by the end of the day?"

"Perhaps," Ijuin said.

"Then possibly you can use them by dark this evening," Shoji said. "I have already asked the Honorable Suzuki to release as many soldiers as possible to help in this endeavor. In fact, he will use every able bodied man in the recently disembarked 1st Division. He has also assured me that he will use anything that floats to help to carry the supplies ashore."

"With such help, we should complete the unloading by daylight tomorrow."

"Good," Shoji said. "I can also tell you that more fighter aircraft from the 331st Kokutai will maintain air cover while you complete your mission. Early this afternoon, they will be relieved by an army fighter squadron from Negros."

"Yes, Admiral."

By 1035 hours, Admiral Ijuin's radio man contacted all ship commanders who replied positively. The vessels had resumed departure positions and all ships could sail at the minimum 20 knots. Ijuin had then, still again, issued the order to sail out of Ormoc Bay. The vessels, including seriously damaged *Okinami,* heaved spirals of smoke as they cut through the water. By noon, Convoy One would be deep in the Camotes Sea.

On the shoreline of Ormoc Bay, Maj. Kusa Imada, CO of the 1st Division's 3rd Battalion, 57th Regiment, mustered his troops and spoke to them. "We have been fortunate," he told his men, "despite the enemy air attacks. Most of our supplies are still safely aboard marus. As soon as we are certain there will be no more enemy air attacks, the marus will return. I have been asked to enlist the aid of every man in this battalion to help in unloading tasks, possibly sometime this evening. All company commanders will therefore rest the men as much as possible so they will be fresh and strong to work throughout the night."

Lt. Minetoshi Yahiro listened carefully to his battalion commander, pleased by the major's words. His C Company would apparently get their supplies after all. He would make a special effort to infuse his men with enthusiasm for the chore of working all night. By morning, they would be fully provisioned and they could march eastward to join the 1st Division's 46th Regiment at Breakneck Ridge in the battle against the Americans.

In the air at this same 1035 hours, Lt. Makase Ibusuki droned southward. He had left Clark Field with 20 Oscars of his 1st Fighter Squadron more than two hours ago and he now approached Ormoc Bay. He had already heard from Lt. Yokoyama who had recounted the heavy air battle over the area.

"We suffered severe losses," the 22nd Squadron commander had told Ibusuki, "but we drove off the enemy with considerable losses to themselves. The Americans have returned to Tacloban to lick their wounds, and you should not meet any new Yankee air formations."

"Nonetheless, we will remain alert," Ibusuki had answered.

Soon, the 20 Oscars of the 1st Fighter Squadron arrived over Ormoc Bay. Soldiers of the 1st Division and sailors aboard Convoy One uttered rousing cheers. They knew that the earlier air cover had mitigated the morning air attack on the convoy, and they assumed that this new squadron of fighter planes would be equally effective.

Lieutenant Ibusuki looked down at the ships that were now sailing westward out of the bay. He next looked at his watch: 1100 hours. Then, he called P/O Arino Kanno. "Arino, you will take your element to the east to keep alert for any more enemy aircraft. I will maintain the first element of fighters from our squadron over the convoy."

"Yes, Lieutenant," Kanno answered.

The Japanese had regained their confidence

after the late afternoon air strikes yesterday and the early morning attack today. They had not suffered badly from the hordes of U.S. air formations. But, at 1130 hours, Adm. Matsuji Ijuin would realize his worst fears, when a swarm of the dreaded B-25 commerce destroyers emerged from the south with a formation of U.S. fighter plane escorts. Further, 16 Lightnings from the 475th Fighter Group were already droning westward to meet and protect the B-25s flying up from Morotai. The Japanese 1st Fighter Squadron would be hard pressed to ward off a skyful of P-47s and P-38s while the skip bombers attacked.

At 1110 hours, the 38th Bomb Group, after crossing the Mindanao Sea, now droned between Cebu and Bohol on the last lap to Ormoc Bay. In the lead B-25, Major McClean looked at his map and then his watch. He called his pilots. "IP in 15 minutes; IP in 15 minutes."

Chapter Eleven

At 1115 hours, Col. Charles MacDonald arrived over Ormoc Bay with his 16 P-38s of the 475th Fighter Group. MacDonald saw no sign of the B-25s coming up from Morotai. However, the colonel saw plenty of enemy planes and he cried into his radio.

"The Mitchells aren't here yet, but there's a bunch of bandits to the north. I'll take them low with our first flights. Johnny," he told Major Loisel, "you take them high with the other flights."

"Okay, Colonel," Loisel answered.

Soon enough, Lt. Makase Ibusuki, commander of the 1st Fighter Squadron, saw the American P-38s in the distance and he too cried into his radio.

"More enemy fighters have arrived from the east. P/O Kanno, you will fly high to attack the rear elements of these Yankee aircraft. I will attack from the west with our first section."

"Yes, Lieutenant," Kannno answered.

Moments later, still another dogfight erupted

over Ormoc Bay. But as usual, the Japanese again lost a lopsided battle. Colonel MacDonald and his wingman bored into a trio of Oscars with raking .50 caliber fire and thumping 37mm shells. The Japanese returned fire, but the American firepower was heavier and the P-38s more durable than the Oscars. While Japanese pilots punctured the P-38 attacks with 7.7mm fire, they failed to seriously damage the Lightnings. In turn, the colonel and his wingman quickly knocked down two Oscars. One Japanese plane exploded from heavy tracing hits, while the second lost a wing and flipped over to crash into the jungles east of Ormoc.

At the high 16,000 feet altitude, Maj. John Loisel and his wingman tangled with a quartet of Oscars under P/O Arino Kanno. Despite the odds, Loisel shattered two of the Oscars, blowing apart the fuselage of one plane with 37mm shells and igniting the fuel tank on the second with raking maching gun fire. Loisel's wingman, meanwhile, successfully riddled away the tail of a third Oscar that fell into the jungle. However, P/O Kanno made a sharp turn and came into the wingman's P-38, shattering the cockpit and killing the pilot before the Japanese pilot arced away.

During the ten minute battle, the Japanese lost seven planes and the Americans two. In the bay, Admiral Ijuin watched from the bridge of cruiser *Kumano* with a mixture of disappointment and relief. Although Lieutenant Ibusuki had lost the air battle, Ijuin noted that these latest interlopers were only fighters. The Americans had apparently spent their fighter-bombers and his convoy was no longer in danger.

However, the 38th Bomb Group had now cleared the channel between Bohol and Cebu Islands and they were flying over the Camotes Sea before going into Ormoc Bay. Maj. Ed McClean, the mission leader, had been scanning the sea below and he suddenly ogled in surprise. Just ahead of him sailed Convoy Two under Cmdr. Noritaru Yatsui. McClean counted two destroyers, three coastal defense ships and a pair of maru transports. The ships were just east of Pori Island and heading northeast toward Ormoc Bay.

McClean frowned. He knew that U.S. planes out of Tacloban had attacked shipping in Ormoc Bay yesterday and probably again this morning. Surely, if the Japanese ships had left the bay, they would have sailed northwest and not into the lower segment of the Camotes Sea. He called Col. Ed Gavin.

"Colonel, what do you make of those ships down there?"

"I don't know if it's part of that Ormoc Bay flotilla. They seem to be sailing north so it may be a separate convoy altogether. Anyway, I suggest you leave a squadron behind to hit them, while the rest of us go into Ormoc Bay."

"Good idea," McClean said. The mission leader called Maj. Ed Maurer of the 405th Squadron. "Ed, take your squadron and hit those ships ahead. I'll ask Major Dunham to leave a flight of P-47s behind to give you cover."

"Okay," Maurer answered McClean.

McClean then called Maj. Bill Dunham, the escort leader. "We've assigned our 405th Squadron to hit those ships below while the rest of us go into Ormoc Bay. I'd like you to leave them some cover."

"Okay," Dunham answered. The 348th Fighter Group major called Capt. Henry Fleischer and asked that he remain behind with 14 P-47s of the 461st Squadron to protect the 405th Bomb Squadron. Dunham, meanwhile, would continue on with the other 20 P-47s to cover the remaining Mitchells of the 38th Group.

On the sea, Commander Yatsui looked in astonishment at the horde of B-25s coming out of the south. The Convoy Two commander could see the protruding nose guns and he had correctly guessed that these low flying Mitchells were dreaded skip bombers. He quickly ordered ships to scatter while destroyer and coastal defense ship AA gunners opened on the enemy bombers.

But even as flak darkened the sky, Maj. Ed Maurer peeled off from his formation with wingman John Henry, dropped near surface level, and skimmed over the water toward destroyer *Hatsuyuki*. Maurer opened with murderous strafing fire from his ten forward firing guns and the .50 caliber tracers ripped the vessel's superstructure. The chattering guns tore up the deck, ignited fires, and scattered AA gunners before the major arced away. Then, within 100 yards of the Japanese ship the trailing Henry unloaded his four 500 pound skip bombs. Two missed, but the other two five second delay fuse bombs hit squarely on the waterline. The American pilot arced away to the left before the bombs exploded in numbing blasts. *Hatsuyuki* quickly listed to port from heavy flooding. However, the ship's commander, Lt. Cmdr. Chiochi Koyama, screamed into his radio.

"You must contain flooding, you must!"

The Japanese sailors worked furiously and sealed the gap, stopping the destroyer from sinking. However, on its ten degree list, *Hatsuyuki* had been slowed to a crawl. Then, Maurer and Henry came back for a second attack on the ship. Now, Henry strafed and Maurer skipped his bombs into the stricken destroyer. Two hits opened more holes and repair crews could no longer contain the flooding and the *Hatsuyuki* went down by the bow, taking most of her crew with her. A coastal defense ship rescued Lieutenant Commander Koyama and 47 other sailors from the destroyer.

Now came Lt. Harry Bradley and his wingman, Lt. Joe Rogers. Bradley ogled with excitement when he saw the fat targets. He skimmed after *Takatsu Maru,* a transport loaded with 30th Division troops. Despite heavy AA fire from accompanying destroyers, the Sunsetter pilot came in low and unleashed heavy .50 caliber fire that ripped up the superstructure and killed hordes of shipboard sailors and soldiers. Then, within a 100 yards of the transport, Lt. Joe Rogers dropped his skip bombs. Three of them slammed into the Japanese ship and the triple explosion enveloped the maru in smoke and flames. *Takatsu Maru* quickly went to the bottom, taking most of the crew and soldier passengers with her.

However, as Bradley and Rogers circled about, Bradley's B-25 caught a solid AA hit from one of the Japanese destroyers, a hit that knocked out the left engine. The plane wobbled and Bradley called Major Maurer. "I'm hit bad. I don't think we can make it back to Morotai."

"Then head for Tacloban," Maurer said. "Keep in contact with ADVON 5th Air Force on your VF channel. If you need to ditch or to bail out, give them your exact position."

"Yes sir," Bradley answered.

But, Bradley could barely get altitude and he called his crews. "Throw everything out that isn't nailed down: ammo, supplies, equipment— everything."

"Yes sir."

After the crew tossed more than a ton of items out of the waist windows, Bradley was able to rise to a 1,000 feet and he nursed his plane towards Tacloban, with Joe Rogers at his side. Two P-47s from the 461st Fighter Squadron accompanied the crippled Mitchell to Tacloban.

Now came Capt. Joe Nelson who roared after a coastal defense vessel. The small warship zigzagged frantically, while its AA gunners fired furiously at the low flying skip bomber. But Nelson had only caught minor shrapnel hits before he loosened shattering .50 caliber forward machine gun fire. The massive strafing barrage chopped away the deck of the small warship and killed at least a dozen sailors before the others darted for cover. Then, again, within 100 yards of *Koshii 110,* Wingman Lt. Jim Cooper released his four skip bombs. One missed, but the other three 500 pounders struck the starboard hull and exploded five seconds later in shattering blasts that badly damaged the coastal defense ship. Moments later, Cooper came in with a strafing run and Nelson released his skip bombs, scoring two more hits. The battered, flaming *Koshii 110* went down with a deafening hiss, leaving a cloud of steam on the water's surface.

Then, Nelson strafed for the last pilot in the 405th Squadron, a Sunsetter who put one skip bomb into transport *Putt Putt Maru.* The blast caused heavy damage on the stern and killed a horde of 30th Division soldiers. However, the maru's crew stopped the flooding and put out flames, so the transport remained afloat.

Thus, the 405th Squadron, with a mere seven planes, had sunk a transport, a coastal defense ship, and a destroyer, while seriously damaging a second transport. Deadly indeed were the 38th Bomb Group's commerce destroyers.

High in the sky, meanwhile, Capt. Henry Fleischer and his 13 P-47 pilots of the 461st Squadron took on a sentai of Zeros out of Del Monte on Mindanao that were covering the Convoy Two. In a matter of minutes, the experienced U.S. pilots with their iron strong Thunderbolts macerated the Japanese air unit.

"Hit them in pairs, in pairs!" Fleischer cried into his radio. "No fancy stuff; our work horses are not as maneuverable as those Zekes."

"Yes sir," Lt. Bill Horton answered.

Fleischer and his wingman began the brawl over the Camotes Sea when they came down at nine o'clock and riddled a flight of Zeros with chattering .50 caliber fire. Two of the planes exploded in hot balls of fire and then flamed into the sea. Lt. Bill Horton got two more Japanese planes in a single pass. His first wing gun burst tore apart a Zero before the fragmented plane tumbled into the Camotes Sea. Even as this first victim fell, Horton opened on a second plane with whooshing 37mm shellfire that blew the Zero apart.

Within five minutes, the 461st Squadron from the 348th Fighter Group downed nine Zeros and damaged four more without a single loss to themselves. The survivors of this Japanese unit out of Del Monte then scattered in several directions.

"Shall we chase after them?" Lieutenant Horton asked.

"No," Fleischer answered. "We'll maintain our cover over these B-25s. Those Nips might send out more fighters."

At 1135 hours, 10 November, the remaining 23 B-25s of the 38th Bomb Group reached Ormoc Bay. Every man aboard every Mitchell gaped in awe at the horde of Japanese ships ahead of them, about a dozen warships and marus. McClean stared for only a fleeting moment before he called Bill Dunham.

"Major, cover us upstairs while we go after those targets."

"Okay," the 460th Fighter Squadron commander answered.

In Ormoc Bay, Adm. Matsuji Ijuin peered in utter shock from the bridge of *Kumano*. He could not believe his eyes: a swarm of B-25s. And, like Commander Yatsui, the admiral also noted on the approaching bombers the forward machine guns protruding from the noses and fuselages. He too realized these enemy planes were the terrifying commerce destroyers. He issued quick orders to his ship commanders.

"Take evasive action! Evasive action! Anti-aircraft gunners will commence fire!" The Convoy One commander then frantically called Manila and spoke to a headquarters aide of the 4th Base Air Force. "Are more fighters on the way?"

"The 1st Squadron of the 331st Kokutai should be there at this time," the aide said, "and Lieutenant Yokoyama will fly out again this afternoon with more aircraft from the 2nd Fighter Squadron."

"We must have aircraft now! At once! We will soon come under attack by the low altitude B-25s with their heavy machine guns and delayed fuse bombs."

"What?" the aide gasped. "That is impossible. There are no such enemy bombers in Leyte."

"They are on the way," Ijuin said, "coming from the south. They apparently made a long flight over the Celebes Sea and the southern Philippines."

"We will send out immediately as many aircraft as possible," the aide said. Meanwhile, Lieutenant

Ibusuki will need to deal with these bombers, while your anti-aircraft gunners do what they can."

Aboard destroyer *Samidare,* Lt. Kiyoshi Kikkawa stared in horrow at the oncoming B-25s. Kikkawa had been in the Pacific war since Guadalcanal, engaging the Americans in the Savo Island battles, the central Solomons contests, and the Central Pacific campaigns. Yet, in none of these fights, despite the prospect of death, had Kikkawa been overly frightened, not even in U.S. Navy dive bombing or torpedo bombing attacks. However, in the East Indies, just before the invasion of the Philippinès, the *Samidare* commander had experienced his first and only B-25 skip bombing attack. The awesome power and deadly accuracy of these commerce destroyers had absolutely terrified him. And now, Kikkawa expected another such devastating experience.

The 38th Bomb Group would not disappoint Lt. Cmdr. Kiyoshi Kikkawa.

Aboard destroyer *Arikaze,* Lt. Koto Madaguchi squinted at the twin engine U.S. bombers in the distance. He had heard of these B-25s with their forward firing machine .guns and delayed fuse bombs, but he had never suffered through a skip bomb attack. Madaguchi, in fact, had considered the stories of these low level devils as gross exaggerations. He did not think that anything could be worse than screaming U.S. navy dive bombers and skimming torpedo bombers.

But, Lt. Kito Madaguchi would soon become a believer.

As Maj. Ed McClean squinted at the zigzagging ships in Ormoc Bay, he cringed instinctively as AA shells from the marus and warships burst about his B-25. The mission commander cried into his radio. "Okay, drop to low level and separate into squadrons. The squadron leaders will then decide when to break off in pairs. The 822nd will go in first, then the 71st, and then the 823rd."

"We read you, Major," Lt. Col. Ed Hawes said.

"Okay, scramble!" McClean cried again.

The 822nd Squadron major went in first with wingman Lt. Cap McLanahan. The two B-25s dropped from their medium altitude to near surface level and roared toward a Japanese destroyer. McClean led to make the strafing attack. But, Convoy One AA fire proved extremely accurate. Before the major reached destroyer *Samidare,* the Japanese gunners struck the trailing McLanahan's Mitchell with two solid flak hits. One explosion tore up the left wing and the second blew apart the cabin, apparently killing McClanahan and his co-pilot instantly. The Mitchell then flipped over and smashed atop the sea, exploding and killing the remainder of the crew.

Maj. Ed McClean had not fared much better. Besides strafing, he also dropped his skip bombs towards *Samidare.* Lt. Cmdr. Kikkawa had deftly veered his destroyer to the right, but one bomb hit, blowing off the destroyer's bow. However, flood crews quickly sealed the breaches. Meanwhile, *Samidare's* gunners riddled the B-25 with flak bursts and shrapnel set McClean's right engine afire, blew up a rear gas tank, knocked off the left engine, and chopped off one of the twin tails. Yet the plane did not explode and McClean miraculously ditched the battered B-25 in the water, skidding to a stop near a remote shoreline.

The crew on this lead 38th Bomb Group Mitchell scrambled out of the plane and flopped into inflated life rafts, taking two injured gunners with them. As the Americans paddled toward shore, they avoided the Japanese in Ormoc Bay and reached a secluded patch of jungle. Within hours, Filippino guerrillas found the six American airmen, nursed them, and eventually got them to Tacloban.

The 822nd Squadron soon lost more planes. As Capt. Bill Franklin and Lt. Harold Sealy skimmed over Ormoc Bay towards a zigzagging maru, heavy AA fire from destroyer *Samidare* and damaged destroyer *Okinami* pummelled the two planes with flak. Neither Mitchell got a chance to strafe or to unload skip bombs. Captain Franklin caught three ack ack hits that ignited the plane. Whooshing flames swept through the aircraft, killing all hands before the plane plopped into the water in a hiss of billowing smoke. Lieutenant Sealy caught flak in both engines and the cabin. Shrapnel killed Sealy and his co-pilot and the plane plopped into the sea. The B-25 quickly sank, taking all six crew members to the bottom.

Rousing cheers exploded amidst the Japanese sailors aboard the two Convoy One warships. However, this quick quartet of kills had not ended the battle. Now came Lt. Jim Fitzsimmons with Ed Gavin on his wing. The two Sunsetters skimmed after a zigzagging coastal defense vessel. The B-25 crews had seen the first four planes of the 822nd Squadron go down and they were tense with fear. Aboard Fitzsimmons' plane, co-pilot Don Raymond stared in awe at the spewing anti-aircraft bursts. Turret gunner Bob Tate licked his dry lips and winced as Fitzsimmons opened with his forward .50 caliber machine guns. Inside the fuselage, waist gunner Roger Cloutier and navigator Joe Gulley felt the sweat dampen their faces, while their nerves grew numb. In the tail, gunner Harry Martin held his triggers tightly, while he ogled at the Japanese ships that zigzagged all over the bay.

The crew had reason to fear. A flak burst suddenly hit Fitzsimmons' plane, ignited one engine, and shuddered the B-25 violently. Next to Fitzsimmons, another flak burst blew open the bomb bay doors on Col. Ed Gavin's plane. But still Fitzsimmons cleared the deck of the coastal defense ship with strafing fire before Gavin dropped skip bombs at masthead height and within 100 yards of *Koshii 31*. One bomb missed, but the other three 500 pounders slammed into the hull, whose superstructure had already been set afire by Fitzsimmons. Five seconds after the hits, three explosions shuddered *Koshii 31* to a stop, opened huge holes in the small warship, and spread hot fires over the superstructure. The coastal defense ship went down quickly, taking most of her crew with her.

"Colonel, sir," Fitzsimmons called Gavin, "I've got one engine out. I don't think I can make it back."

"Fly on to Tacloban."

"Yes sir."

Fitzsimmons arced his crippled plane out of the bay and then headed eastward toward Leyte, while Col. Ed Gavin banked his plane to the left to begin the long flight back to Morotai.

Now came the last two planes of the 822nd Squadron, the Mitchells of Lt. Ed Polanski and Lt. Allen White. The Sunsetters skimmed after destroyer *Hatsuhara* that had been slightly damaged by the 110th Recon Squadron earlier this morning. Both Mitchells sustained damage from anti-aircraft bursts that opened holes in their wings and fuselages. However, the planes continued on. Polanski sent chattering .50 caliber fire from ten forward guns into the destroyer, shattering the superstructure, starting fires, and scattering Japanese crews. Then White came within a 100 yards of the destroyer and released four skip bombs. Unfortunately, thick black AA smoke had obscured Allen's view and only one 500 pounder hit. The explosion, however, opened a hole in the stern and sea water poured into the aft. Japanese sailors stopped the flooding, but not before *Hatsuhara* listed badly and slowed to a crawl.

Then, as the two B-25s arced away from target, more anti-aircraft fire from destroyer *Samidare* hit Polanski's plane. The B-25 jolted four times in quick succession and then slid downward to the right. Shrapnel had ripped out the bottom of the fuselage and cut oil lines to drop pressure in the right engine. The hit had also left a six foot hole in the right wing.

Polanski frantically called his crew. "Report damage and casualties!"

Radio gunner Fred Hellman answered first. "Sir, we've got the bottom ripped out and Lieutenant Gulley is hurt bad, bleeding heavily."

"Goddamn it," Polanski cursed. He also called Colonel Gavin. "Sir, we're all shot up; we can never make it back to Morotai."

"Have you got your engines working?" the colonel asked.

"One of them, sir. I'll need to feather the right engine. I think I've got shattered elevators."

"Try to make it to Tacloban."

"Yes sir."

Thus the 822nd Squadron of the 38th Bomb Group had suffered a horrible run. Four planes had gone down: Maj. Ed McClean, Lt. Cap McLanahan, Lt. Harold Sealy, and Lt. Bill Franklin. Two cripples were sputtering toward Tacloban: Lt. Jim Fitzsimmons and Lt. Ed. Polanski. Col. Ed Gavin's plane was damaged, but the Sunsetter commander would nurse the B-25 back to Morotai. Only Allen White had escaped unscathed. For these losses and damage, the 822nd Squadron had sunk a coastal defense ship and damaged a destroyer.

Adm. Matsuji Ijuin was ecstatic. The first formation of skip bombers had not hurt him as badly as he might have expected. He turned to his communications officer. "You will order all commanders to continue evasive action. You will also order all anti-aircraft gunners to remain on full alert for new attacks."

"Yes, Honorable Ijuin."

"If we are as successful against the next group of B-25 low flying bombers we may yet escape with the bulk of our vessels. Our gunners are to be congratulated for their bravery and accuracy."

"Yes, Admiral," the aide said again.

Aboard destroyer *Arikaze,* Lt. Koto Madaguchi had been watching the air attacks with a mixture of surprise and satisfaction. He had not been impressed by the skimming B-25 skip bombers. His AA gunners had shot down at least two of the attacking Mitchells with no harm to his own destroyer or to any of the marus. He thus believed that the stories of these skip bombers were indeed an exaggeration.

But the Americans were not stupid. Lt. Col. Ed Hawes, now technically in command of the remaining 38th Bomb Group units, had carefully evaluated the results so far. He concluded that the 822nd Squadron had come in low too long and over too much open sea, thus allowing the Japanese to concentrate massive anti-aircraft fire for a long period of time before the Mitchells reached target range. So Hawes would change tactics. He called John Irick.

"Captain, take your 823rd Squadron to the east, circle around Ormoc and come into the bay over the mountains from the northeast. I'll take the 71st Squadron and come into the bay over the mountains from the east. If we come in from the landward side, we'll be right on top of those ships before they can throw too much ack ack at us."

"Yes sir, Colonel," Irick answered.

The sailors aboard Convoy One saw the B-25s suddenly veer to the eastward and fly over the ridges beyond Ormoc. The bridge officer on *Kumano* stared in surprise. "Honorable Ijuin, have the American bombers broken off their attack?"

"It appears so," Ijuin grinned. "They saw what happened to their first formation of bombers. Our excellent gunners shot down most of their aircraft. The Yankee dogs have obviously had enough."

"Let us hope so, Admiral."

"I am sure," the admiral gestured. "Reform the vessels so the flotilla may get underway."

"Yes, Admiral."

But in a few minutes, Adm. Matsuji Ijuin would be in for the shock of his life.

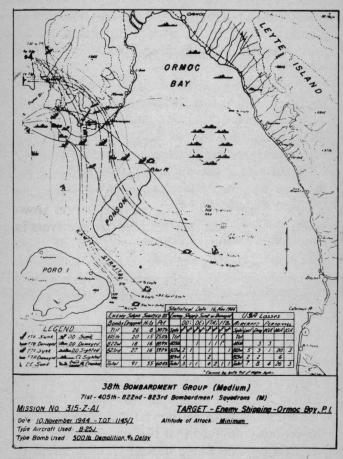

This map shows how the 38th Bomb Group skip bombers hit
Japanese ships from east of Pori Island into Ormoc Bay.

Chapter Twelve

As Lt. Col. Ed Hawes and his fellow airmen of the 38th Bomb group prepared to attack Convoy One, the dogfights overhead continued. Col. Charles MacDonald and his P-38 pilots from the 475th Fighter Group had already fragmented Lt. Makase Ibusuki's 1st Fighter Squadron, shooting down 7 planes and damaging three more. However, Ibusuki rallied his ten scattered survivors in the hope of downing at least some of these Mitchells from the other Sunsetter squadrons. Further, 24 Jack fighter planes arrived to join Ibusuki. Lt. Yonosoki Iguchi had returned to the battle area with his 352nd Sentai.

Capt. Mutohara Okamura, CO of the 22nd Air Brigade, continued to show a remarkable foresight. The battle tested, combat experienced Japanese air leader was perhaps the most skeptical officer in the Philippines. He knew that the Americans had grown powerful in strength, and he seriously doubted that two or even three raids on Convoy One would deplete U.S. air strength. He had fully expected the Americans to unleash squadron after squadron of planes on the ships in Ormoc Bay. Thus Okamura had sent out still more aircraft under Lieutenant Iguchi to intercept new American air formations that tried to attack the Japanese vessels.

And, as soon as Lieutenant Anabuki returned with his riddled 351st Sentai, Okamura also ordered him to fly out again as soon as possible. "You will find as many aircraft and pilots as possible and return to Ormoc Bay within the hour."

"Our pilots are exhausted, Honorable Okamura," Anabuki complained.

"So are the Americans, so are our ground troops on Leyte, and our sailors in Ormoc Bay," Okamura answered sharply. "We are all in need of rest, but the fight must go on. These marus must be protected so they can deliver these much needed supplies to our soldiers."

"Yes, Honorable Okamura," Anabuki said. "I will muster twenty aircraft and leave Bacolod Field as soon as possible."

"Good," the 22nd Air Brigade commander answered.

However, neither the reformed remnants of Lieutenant Ibusuki's squadron, the recently arrived 24 Jacks of the 352nd Sentai, nor the later arrival of Lieutenant Anabuki's 351st Sentai would get a chance to hit the 38th Bomb Group skip bombers. Not only was Col. Charles Mac-Donald still hovering over Ormoc Bay with his Lightning pilots of the 432nd Squadron, but Maj. Bill Dunham had now arrived with 24 P-47s from the 384th Fighter Group.

"How can we help out, Colonel?" Dunham asked MacDonald.

"Take those Jacks that just came from the west, probably out of Negros," the 475th Fighter Group commander answered. "We'll take anything that comes from the north."

"Roger," Dunham answered.

Then, Dinghy Dunham took his airmen high and soon came down on the Japanese 352nd Sentai. The major ogled at the formation of enemy planes for this had been the first time he had seen an entire squadron of the new, speedy Jacks. He called his pilots. "Be careful, goddamn careful; those Nip planes are fast, so you'll need to be exceptionally alert."

"Yes sir," Lt. Tom Sheet said.

The 460th Squadron pilots roared into the Jacks with their much sturdier P-47s which could take plenty of punishment. The heavy Thunderbolt power proved too much for the celebrated new Jacks. Maj. Bill Dunham and his wingman raked two Jacks with heavy .50 caliber fire that chopped open the fuselage on one plane and hewed off the wing of a second. Both Japanese fighters plopped into the sea. Two more Jacks tried to outrun Lt. Tom Sweet and his wingman, but the two American pilots opened throttle and their Thunderbolts caught up to the Japanese. Streaking machine gun fire and 37mm shells knocked both planes apart and sent the Jacks flaming into the sea.

Other 460th Squadron pilots proved equally

adept. The Americans continually chased Jacks, outrunning them, outshooting them, and out-driving them. When P-47 pilots got astern of a Jack their heavy fire usually destroyed the enemy plane. However, when a Jack pilot tailed a Thunderbolt, the chattering 7.7mm fire only peppered holes in the bull hide P-47, rarely causing serious damage, much less destroying the U.S. fighter plane. Lieutenant Iguchi and his 352nd Sentai pilots felt utter frustration with their inability to knock down the strongly constructed Thunderbolts, while their own Jacks continued to fall out of the sky.

Within ten minutes, Iguchi lost nine fighters and serious damage to five more. The Japanese Sentai leader could not even get near a B-25.

To the north, Lieutenant Ibusuki had rallied pilots, but the effort became an exercise in futility. 475th Fighter Group pilots pummelled the 1st Squadron that was now outnumbered two to one. Within minutes, the P-38 airmen shot six more Oscars out of the air. MacDonald got another kill when he chopped apart an Oscar with ripping .50 caliber machine gun fire, and Maj. John Loisel got his second kill of the day when he blew away an Oscar cockpit with telling 37mm shell hits.

By noon, the two Japanese fighter units had been routed and their survivors chased off. Now, the U.S. fighter pilots simply loitered in the sky over Ormoc Bay.

On the surface of the bay, Matsuji Ijuin had been watching the air battles. Each passing moment had worsened the admiral's dismay since he saw one Japanese plane after another fall out of the sky. Still, while he regretted these obviously high aircraft losses, he hoped there would be no more air attacks on his ships. The B-25s had disappeared to the east and the U.S. planes above were fighters and not fighter-bombers. He ordered his commanders to get underway, the third time he had done so this morning.

But Ijuin would suffer the ultimate disaster.

The Convoy One commander jerked when he heard heavy, low altitude aircraft drones to the north. He squinted from the bridge of *Kumano* and then stiffened as low flying B-25s suddenly emerged over the mountains of Northwest Leyte. The admiral gaped and yelled to his radio officer.

"Alert all gunners!"

"Yes, Admiral."

But, this time, the Convoy One AA personnel did not get enough time to fire for several minutes at the approaching planes. Ed Hawes had guessed right in coming in suddenly from the landward side. His planes from the 71st Squadron, in pairs, were already within strafing range of the Japanese ships that now zigzagged frantically to escape the skip bombers. Hawes and his wingman, Lt. Joe Adams, roared toward destroyer *Okinami* that had shot down two B-25s from the 822nd Squadron. This time, the destroyer's flak gunners could not hit the two streaking Mitchells before Hawes opened with shattering .50 caliber machine guns. The overwhelming firepower raked the deck, killing hordes of men, starting fires, and forcing the flak gunners to cover.

Okinami's crew scattered as Hawes arced away and Adams continued toward the ship at masthead height. Within 100 yards, the lieutenant released his skip bombs, four of them, and then banked his B-25 to the left. Several seconds later, four numbing explosions rocked the destroyer before fires erupted through every part of the hull.

"We got her, Colonel, we got her," Adams cried into his radio.

"We'll get her again," Hawes answered.

A moment later, Adams strafed the burning decks of the destroyer before Hawes dropped his skip bombs. He scored with two that blew more holes in the hull. *Okinami* listed badly, while flames raged out of control. The destroyer's sailors abandoned ship, leaping into the bay. Within minutes the Japanese tin can fell on its side, capsized, and went to the bottom of Ormoc Bay.

Then, Capt. Bob Blair and his wingman, Lt. Joe Bellanger, skimmed toward a transport. Blair stared at the big zigzagging *Kata Maru* that sent up furious anti-aircraft fire. The ship lay heavy in the water and Blair guessed that the vessel was heavily loaded with supplies as well as troops. The captain picked up his radio.

"Let's take the fat one, Joe."

"I'm with you," Bellanger answered, following the captain in close tandem.

Bob Blair opened with blistering .50 caliber strafing fire from his ten forward firing guns. The heavy blasts chipped away the superstructure, killed sailors and officers, and smashed equipment. As soon as the captain arced away, Lt. Bellanger released his skip bombs and also arced away. One 500 pounder skidded past the stern of *Katu Maru,* but the other three hit squarely. Numbing explosions rocked the transport while igniting three fires. The two pilots then circled, with Bellanger now raking the ship with strafing fire before Blair scored two skip bomb hits, tearing the ship asunder. Within minutes, *Katu Maru* settled under the surface of the sea and fell to the bottom. Most of her crew went with her.

As Blair and Bellanger circled about the sky to watch *Katu Maru* go under, they saw three launch boats puttering out from shore to pick up the floundering sailors.

"Let's get 'em," Blair said.

"I've still got plenty of rounds," Bellanger answered.

A moment later, the two 71st Squadron pilots once more zoomed over the surface of the sea and sent chattering tracer fire into the barges. The small craft quickly sank. Then, Blair and Bellanger banked away to climb high.

Now came the other three planes of the 71st Squadron. The B-25s streaked over the bay, unleashing heavy machine gun fire that struck *Koshio Maru* and coastal defense ship *Koshii 32* of Convoy One and *Koshii 43* of Convoy Two that had escorted the ships from Mindanao. However, heavy ack ack fire blew away the left wing of one B-25 that upended and splashed into the sea. The crew perished in the downed skip bomber. AA gunners from Convoy One also damaged the other two B-25s, riddling the tail on one Mitchell and knocking out the right engine of the second.

Still, the three Mitchells scored four skip bomb hits. One 500 bomber damaged *Koshio Maru* and another hit set afire coastal defense ship *Koshio 32*. Capt. Sam Cole scored squarely with two skip bomb hits on destroyer *Hatsuhara*. The explosions opened the aft of the Japanese warship in uncontrollable cascades. The destroyer went down by the stern.

Thus in a matter of minutes, two destroyers and a transport were down and three more ships damaged. Inside cruiser *Kumano's* communications room, Admiral Ijuin screamed into his radio. "Where are the escorting aircraft? Where? And why have not our anti-aircraft gunners destroyed this new formation of B-25s?"

But, no one could answer the Convoy One commander. And in fact, he had bearly stopped barking when he heard the heavy drones of planes again, this time from the east. A moment later, another swarm of B-25s loomed from the land areas beyond Ormoc Bay. And again, before AA gunners on the scattered ships could effectively attack the Mitchells, the skip bombers had brought their forward firing guns within range.

As Capt. John Irick and wingman Charles Musick of the 823rd Squadron skimmed over the bay, Irick ogled at the heavy ack ack fire spewing up from the Japanese ships. He felt a mixture of fear and resentment. He had been in combat a long time and he wondered what he was doing here. Why had he joined the Air Corps? Why had he put himself in this kind of position? Not only to endanger his own life, but also the lives of a crew that depended on him. All he could tell himself: this was the silliest thing he had ever done. But then, his face hardened and he flew on with determination.

Irick opened with chattering machine gun fire against damaged *Koshio Maru*. The heavy tracers ignited tons of supply on the ship's deck. But as the trailing Musick neared *Koshio,* an AA hit chopped out a chunk of the B-25s wing and his skip bombs went awry. However, Irick turned quickly and roared back after the ship again. He released two skip bombs that slammed squarely into the starboard quarter of his target, and seconds later two thunderous explosions cut the 10,000 ton maru in two. The twisted vessel quickly sank in a huge balloon of hissing fire and smoke.

Now, Capt. Zane Corbin and wingman Capt. Luke Lupardus came into the bay. Corbin looked at the big cruiser that sent up a wall of ack ack. Then, he called Lupardus. "Luke, let's get the big one. Are you game?"

"I'm with you, Zane," Lupardus answered.

The two Sunsetter pilots dropped low and raced towards cruiser *Kumano* in tandem. As Corbin pressed his machine gun buttons, he got no response. His guns had jammed. Meanwhile, a flak hit twisted the bomb bay doors on Lupardus's plane and he could not release his bombs. Both pilots arced way before Lupardus called Corbin.

"I can't drop bombs."

"And I can't strafe," Corbin said. "Okay,

Luke, you strafe and I'll bomb."

"Follow me," Lupardus answered.

Lupardus opened on the zigzagging *Kumano* with heavy machine gun fire, despite the ack ack bursting all about him. The raking fire from his ten guns chased the sailors to cover, including Admiral Ijuin. As soon as Lupardus arced away, Zane Corbin was on top of the big warship. He released his four bombs from less than 75 yards away. But as he arced away, his B-25 caught a flak burst that chopped a five foot hole in his right wing and destroyed his radio. However, seconds later, four booming explosions almost bounced the big cruiser out of the water, while jerking Corbin's damaged B-25 more than 100 feet higher in altitude. All four of Corbin's bombs had struck solidly.

When the captain arced his plane about for a look, he saw the big warship burning furiously and listing badly. Hundreds of Japanese sailors were leaping into the sea.

"Goddamn, Captain," the co-pilot said, "we got her."

"We sure did," Corbin answered with a grin.

Aboard *Kumano,* Admiral Ijuin could not believe that his Convoy One flagship was going down. He stood immobile on the bridge, squinting at the raging fires, coughing from the dense smoke, and staring at the horde of men leaping over the side. His aide pleaded with him.

"We must abandon ship, Admiral, we must."

For a moment, Ijuin remained in shock, but he finally nodded. "Yes, we must abandon ship," he said softly.

Even as Ijuin left the sinking cruiser more of his vessels suffered fatal hits. As Lt. Jim Corn and his wingman came into Ormoc Bay, the two Sunsetter pilots saw an array of burning, smoking, zig-zagging, sinking ships. Corn could not tell which vessels were going down and which were still afloat. But he finally singled out the undamaged transport *Kozo Maru*. In the tumultuous confusion that now prevailed in the bay, Corn and his wingman met only sporadic AA fire that caused no problems. The two 823rd Squadron pilots carried out two attacks on the transport with sweeping machine gun fire and skidding skip bombs. Four of the eight 500 pounders slammed into the ship and the array of booming explosions knocked the maru apart. Within a few minutes, *Kozo Maru* went down, taking tons of supplies and most of her crew with her.

Aboard destroyer *Arikaze,* Lt. Kito Madaguchi looked in horror at the wanton destruction around him. He rightly feared that he would become a target himself. Soon enough, two B-25 skip bombers came after him. However, dense smoke from burning ships, exploding AA, and a smoke screen had obscured *Arikaze* and only one of the four skip bombs hit, opening a hole in the aft. Fortunately, repair crews sealed the breach, but not before the ship fell into a ten degree list, with its stern awash.

By 1230 hours, the skip bombing attack was over. The Sunsetter's 405th Squadron had decimated Convoy Two, sinking coastal defense vessel *Koshio 110* and transport *Takatsu Maru,* while damaging other ships. The other Sunsetter squadrons had macerated Convoy One. Flag cruiser *Kumano* along with destroyers *Okinami* and *Hatsuhara* were down or going down. Coastal defense ship *Koshi 31* was down as were transports *Kozu Maru, Katu Maru* and *Kashio Maru.*

A mere 30 B-25s from the 38th Bomb Group had thus sunk five warships and four marus, while damaging several others, most of them quite seriously. The commerce destroyers had once more shown their terrifying effectiveness against surface ships. In fact, never in the Pacific war had so few bombers sunk and damaged so many large ships in so short a time as had these 38th Bomb Group skip bombers.

Admiral Ijuin, Commander Yatsui, and Lieutenant Commander Kikkawa had justifiably gaped in horror when they first saw the 38th Bomb Group commerce destroyers coming after them. Skeptics like Lieutenant Madaguchi had become sober believers. The Sunsetters' strafing, skip bombing B-25s were indeed the most awesome weapon ever used against surface ships.

Still, the Sunsetters had paid dearly for their stunning victory. They had lost five planes, suffered grave damage to four more planes that were trying to make Tacloban, and moderate to heavy damage on 12 other B-25s that were sputtering back to Morotai. Five other planes had suffered light damage. Only four B-25s had escaped unscathed. The 38th Bomb Group would count 33 casualties from this mission, including 26 MIAs, three KIAs, and four WIAs. Never in its three years of combat had the Sunsetters experienced such high losses on one mission.

For the Japanese, of course, bedlam now prevailed on the surface of Ormoc Bay and the Camotes Sea. The crews on surviving ships of Convoys One and Two were hard pressed to put out fires, repair damage, seal breaches, treat wounded, and rescue survivors. Rescuers had plucked Admiral Ijuin himself from the sea and taken him aboard destroyer *Samidare* where he now maintained his flag.

"We can no longer hope to discharge anything at Ormoc," the admiral said to Lieutenant Commander Kikkawa. "We can do nothing but return to Manila. You will form all ships into pattern at once."

"Yes, Admiral," Kikkawa said.

But, Ijuin's troubles were not yet over.

At 1330 hours, a new swarm of aircraft loomed from the south, the 14 P-38s of the 70th Fighter Squadron, 18th Fighter Group. The Lightnings, carrying 1,000 pound bombs, had left Wama Field on Noemfoor, New Guinea, at 1015 hours and they had now reached the smoking battle area. Maj. Bill Cowper, the mission leader, looked in astonishment at the devastation in Ormoc Bay. He could not tell which ships were undamaged because every ship on the surface appeared to be burning or sinking. He called his pilots.

"Okay, try to find a worthwhile target and go after it."

"Yes sir," Lt. Bob Mitchell said.

The 14 Lightnings roared down on the scattered ships. They met little ack ack fire from the 1st Transportation Fleet sailors, while the 475th and 348th Fighter Groups pilots had killed all enthusiasm among the surviving 4th Base Air Force fighter pilots.

Cowper and his wingman, Lt. Ellis Bentley, came down on damaged destroyer *Shiranuhi,* first strafing and then dropping a pair of thousand pounders. The bombs hit the ship squarely, smashed the superstructure, and shuddered the vessel to a stop. A moment later, two more P-38s laced the Japanese destroyer with bombs. More explosions opened two huge holes in the hull and water poured into the stricken ship. *Shiranuhi* slowly capsized and sank to the bottom of Ormoc Bay.

Next came Lt. Bob Mitchell and his wingman, Lt. James Glenny. They dove on the transport *Putt Putt Maru* of Convoy Two. First, they raked the deck with strafing fire and then hit the vessel with two 1,000 pound bombs that ignited fires on the main deck. The next two P-38s whacked the ship again and the maru, jammed with 30th Division troops, went down quickly. The transport took most of her soldier passengers with her.

Other 70th Fighter Squadron pilots also scored, damaging another destroyer, another coastal defense ship, and the lone surviving transport, *Kinka Maru.*

Then, a squadron of Oscars suddenly emerged from the west, the 351st Sentai under Lt. Satashi

Anabuki. Lt. Ellis Bentley saw them first and he quickly called Bill Cowper. "Major, a swarm of bandits coming on."

"Okay," Cowper answered. "We've already done all the dive bombing we could. All pilots, climb high, stick to your wingmen, and come down on those Japanese planes in pairs."

"Yes sir," Lt. Bob Mitchell answered.

Moments later, the last dogfight of the day erupted over Ormoc Bay. Again, the more experienced Americans in their superior P-38s mauled still another Japanese fighter formation. Within five minutes, Cowper and his 70th Squadron pilots of the 18th Fighter Group knocked down nine Oscars and damaged four more to a loss of two P-38s. Cowper himself knocked down two planes with machine gun fire and 37mm shells. Lieutenants Bentley, Mitchell, and Glenney had also scored.

By 1345 hours, the battle was over. Lieutenant Anabuki limped back to Negros Island with his 351st Sentai survivors. Meanwhile, Admiral Ijuin and Commander Yatsui mustered their surface ship survivors, a mere seven vessels out of 22 ships that had left Manila and Cagayan. No supplies reached the Japanese 1st Division and no 30th Division reinforcements reached Baybay on Leyte. The Japanese had suffered a disaster against the U.S. 5th Air Force, especially from the 38th Bomb Group skip bombing attack. Besides the heavy loss in ships, the Japanese had also lost 110 planes during the past 24 hours.

After the battle, wild excitement prevailed at

Tacloban, despite the heavy work for ground crews. The fighter planes of the 348th and 18th Groups had come in to land and refuel before returning to New Guinea. Also, the damaged B-25s of the 38th Bomb Group were trying to land, as were the returning fighters of the 475th and 49th Groups that were based at Tacloban.

Col. Dan Hutchinson and Col. Lief Sverdrup had mustered every available man to cope with the heavy traffic about the single airfield. "Get 'em gassed up quick and send them on their way," Hutchinson told his service chiefs. "We just don't have the room to hold all those planes in revetment areas."

"Yes sir."

Sverdrup and his 28th Air Depot personnel also worked quickly. They set up bucket brigade systems: planes landing, led off the runway, quickly serviced and refueled. Gen. Ennis Whitehead had watched the frantic activity with one of his rare grins.

"Goddamn, we sure did them in this time."

"Yes sir," his aide said.

"Make sure those flyers get everything they need," Whitehead gestured.

By late afternoon, mess crews had fed every visiting airman a hot meal before they and their aircraft returned to bases in Morotai, Sansapor, and Noemfoor. By dark, Tacloban returned to normal. Lieutenant Fitzsimmons, Lt. Ed Polanski, Capt. Zane Corbin and other Sunsetters who came into Tacloban for repairs were on the way back to Morotai. Similarly, the P-47 pilots of the

460th and 461th Squadrons and the P-38 pilots of the 70th Squadron were also on their way home to bases in Noemfoor and Sansapor.

Far to the north, in Manila, General Yamashita, Adm. Akira Shoji, and Gen. Kyoji Tominga listened soberly to the discouraging reports of losses at Ormoc Bay: hundreds of troops, countless tons of supplies, 15 surface ships, and more than a 100 aircraft. Yamashita looked at Tominga.

"We must have a new effort. You must send out every plane that can fly to protect Convoy Three that now sails toward Ormoc."

"I assure you, Honorable Yamashita, the flotilla will safely reach Leyte," the 4th Base Air Force CinC answered. "While we suffered heavy losses, we also administered severe losses to the enemy. Our pilots report that dozens of American fighter planes were shot down and almost all of the B-25 low altitude bombers were destroyed. The Americans have expended themselves in these attacks on the first two convoys. They cannot mass aircraft to attack Admiral Matsuyama."

Yamashita looked at Admiral Shoji. "Well?"

"I am inclined to agree with General Tominga," the 1st Transportation Fleet commander said. "While the honorable Suzuki may not get everything he wants, a full combat division and their supplies will surely be invaluable to aid him in the Leyte struggle. Also, since we fortunately disembarked the 1st Division troops before the American attacks, we will only need to supply them when conditions are favorable."

Honorable Yamashita,'' Tominga said, ''we have learned that utter chaos now prevails at Tacloban. The air field is a mass of confusion. Dozens of damaged Yankee aircraft have attempted to land there and many planes have crashed, blocking and gouging the runway. I see no possibility of any new enemy air attacks on Convoy Three before Admiral Matsuyama arrives safely at Ormoc this afternoon.''

"Good," Yamashita said. However, there was a tinge of doubt in his voice.

And in fact, the 14th Army Group CinC had reason to feel doubt. The powerful U.S. Navy TF 38 carrier fleet would take over where the U.S. Army's 5th Air Force had left off.

Chapter Thirteen

By dawn of 11 November 1944, Convoy Three had cleared Masbate Island and now sailed through the southern area of the Sibuyan Sea. Adm. Muto Matsuyama, the most successful admiral in the 1st Transportation Fleet's Manila-Leyte Express runs, stood on the bridge of flag destroyer *Hamani*. He stared at the other ships of his convoy, six more destroyers, three of which carried troops, two coastal defense ships, and five marus. They carried 12,000 men of the 26th Division and 6,600 tons of supplies. Matsuyama had seen the American PBY scout planes yesterday, but no American planes had been over his convoy since then.

Matsuyama had learned of the disaster to Convoys One and Two in Ormoc Bay and the Camotes Sea, and he had also heard of the alleged U.S. air losses in these attacks. Admiral Shoji had assured the Convoy Three commander that the Americans, now spent, could not launch new attacks until they brought in new air replacements. Matsuyama also knew that the American carrier fleet had been last seen retiring eastward toward Saipan for apparent rest and replenishment. Finally, since Matsuyama had not seen enemy scout planes for the past 18 hours or more, he felt quite confident of reaching Ormoc without damage.

An aide came next to the flotilla commander interrupting his meditations. "Excuse the intrusion, Honorable Matsuyama. I have a message from Manila."

"Yes?"

"They say we can expect a squadron of fighters to begin its convoy air cover at 0700 hours."

"Good," Matsuyama said. However, the news did not excite the admiral one way or another, for he expected no American air attacks. Matsuyama could not have been more wrong.

The U.S. TF 38 carrier force, after a speedy 30 hour voyage, had now reached a point only 200 miles east of San Bernadino Strait that separated Legaspi and Samar Islands. At 0600 hours, Adm. Fred Sherman launched search planes, while deck crews aboard the fast carriers readied more than 300 planes. The TF 38 commander had ordered his scout planes to comb an area from 025° to 230° to a distance of 350 miles. After the search planes had been out for an hour, probing the waters of the Sibuyan Sea, Sherman grew impatient. He paced nervously on the bridge of flag carrier *USS Essex,* squinting to the west or looking at the swarm of AG 4 aircraft jammed on the flight deck below.

"We'll find them, sir," Sherman's aide said.

The admiral nodded, but he continued to pace the metal deck, drinking coffee and nibbling on a roll. The deck crews below also grew restless, occasionally staring up at the bridge to wait for take off orders. Finally, at 0700 hours a positive report reached *Essex*.

"Enemy convoy of seven destroyers, two destroyer escorts, and five merchant ships in the Sibuyan Sea, approximate position of 11 degrees north by 123.4 degrees west. Sailing southwest on a 210 degree course at about 20 knots."

"That means those ships are about eight hours from their destination," the aide told the TF 38 commander.

"Okay, launch planes," Sherman said.

"Yes sir."

Men on the *Essex* carrier deck cheered when the signal flags went up at 0745 hours. Sailors rushed about swiftly, warming up planes, clearing decks, and helping pilots and crews into their aircraft.

By 0800 hours, Cmdr. Jim Mini, CO of AG 4 sat in his Dauntless dive bomber and revved his engine. At 0810 hours, the launch officer dropped his flag and Mini roared off the flight deck of *Essex*. Eleven more Dauntlesses followed him. Moments later, Lt. Cmdr. Vince Lambert with wingmen Lt. Art Singer and Lt. Jim Collins also roared off the deck, with nine more Dauntlesses following them.

Finally, Cmdr. Dave McCampbell, the greatest U.S. Navy fighter ace in the Pacific, taxied into position to take off in his VF 4 lead Hellcat. McCampbell had already downed more then 30

219

enemy planes during two tours of combat and he hoped to raise his score even higher. By the time McCampbell finished combat, he would be the greatest air ace in U.S. Navy history with 34 kills.

McCampbell stiffened when the launch flag dropped and seconds later he zoomed down the deck and out to sea. Fifteen more Hellcat fighters of VF 4 followed him. Soon, the 38 planes from *Essex* jelled into formation to lead the first strike force on the Japanese Convoy Three.

Other planes from TG 38.3 also zoomed off carrier decks: 12 fighters and 12 torpedo bombers from *USS Langley* under Lt. Cmdr. Ed Craig; 12 fighters, 12 torpedo bombers, and 12 dive bombers from *USS Ticonderoga* under Lt. Cmdr. Ed Anderson.

At 0900 hours, 24 Oscars from the Japanese 1st Fighter Squadron still hung over Convoy Three that had now reached the last stretch of the Sibuyan Sea before cutting sharply into the Camotes Sea and then into Ormoc Bay. Lt. Makase Ibusuki had kept a four plane flight under P/O Arino Kanno to the east to keep an eye out for American planes. Ibusuki knew that American snooper aircraft had been over the convoy a couple of hours ago, and he had taken this precaution. At 0910 hours, Kanno saw the horde of U.S. carrier planes heading toward the Sibuyan Sea. The Oscar scout leader quickly called Ibusuki.

"Lieutenant, enemy carrier planes approaching. They are flying westward through San Bernadino Strait, and they obviously intend to attack the convoy."

"We will attack them at once," the 1st Squadron commander said.

But 24 Oscars were no match for 36 U.S. Navy Hellcats that were manned by such combat honed pilots as Dave McCampbell.

Cmdr. Jim Mini, leading this first TF 38 strike, saw the Japanese Oscars coming toward them and he quickly called his fighter leader. "Dave, take the fighter planes out ahead and hit those bandits."

"Okay, Jim," McCampbell answered.

Moments later, the 36 Hellcats of TG 38.3 clashed with the 24 Oscars. The battle would end in still another lopsided American victory. Dave McCampbell himself got three kills in less than a minute when he downed a trio of Oscars with sweeping .50 caliber wing fire. He chopped the tail off one plane, shattered the cockpit of a second 1st Squadron aircraft, and ignited the gas tank on the third. All three enemy planes tumbled downward and crashed into the sea.

Other fighter pilots from carriers *Essex, Langley,* and *Ticonderoga* also scored. Within ten minutes, the U.S. airmen downed ten more Oscars and damaged another three. 1st Squadron survivors then darted away, leaving the way clear for the U.S. Navy bombers. On the surface of the Sibuyan Sea, Adm. Muto Matsuyama looked up in horror at the approaching American planes.

"Quickly, take evasive action! All gunners, attack these enemy aircraft at once, at once!"

"Yes, Admiral."

Whoop alarms echoed across the decks of the 14

ships in Convoy Three. Japanese helmsmen spun wheels and assumed zigzag courses. Gunners leaped into gun pits and crews battened down equipment and supplies. However, despite the snaking movement of the Japanese ships and the AA fire the Americans scored heavily.

Cmdr. Jim Mini cried into his TBS. "Okay, hit them in pairs, in pairs! Take the marus first; we want the merchant ships right away."

"Yes sir," Lt. Cmdr. Vince Lambert answered.

Moments later, Mini came down on oiler *Jinei Maru* with three more dive bombers in this first flight. The oiler's helmsman tried frantically to avoid the American Dauntlesses, but Mini did not waver in his glide dive and he soon dropped a pair of 500 pounders. Both hit and exploded, erupting fire and smoke. Within the next half minute, three more 500 pounders struck the oiler. More explosions erupted when fires ignited the stored oil. The ship almost blew apart and went down quickly in a huge hiss of steam. Most of her crew went down with the 10,000 ton *Jinei Maru*.

The other eight bombers from *Essex* singled out other ships in the convoy. Two bombs struck coastal defense ship *Koshii 22*, causing raging fires, although the ship did not sink. Other bombs struck destroyers *Wakatsuki* and *Maki*, damaging their superstructures.

Now came the *Essex* torpedo bombers. Lt. Cmdr. Vince Lambert went after the fat transport, 10,000 ton *Kamoi Maru*, that was jammed with 26th Division troops. Lambert called his two wingmen. "Okay, let's make our torpedoes count."

"We're with you," Lt. Art Singer answered.

The three U.S. Avengers weathered heavy ack ack fire and held a steady course, streaking towards the zigzagging transport. Within 500 yards of the maru, Lambert, Singer, and Lt. Joe Collins dropped their torpedoes. All three fish ran straight for the big ship. *Kamoi's* helmsman maneuvered desperately away from the torpedoes, but he could not avoid them all. As Lambert and his wingmen banked away, a numbing blast jerked their Avengers. When Lambert took a look, he saw raging fires. Moments later, four more Avengers came after the transport and dropped a new quartet of torpedoes, two of which hit. More dense smoke rose from the victim. *Kamoi Maru* quickly listed and began a swift descent to the bottom, even as sailors and hundreds of soldiers leaped over the side. The big transport went down with most of her crew and passengers.

The other torpedo bombers from *Essex* roared after other ships in the convoy, scoring hits on destroyers *Nagamo, Shimikaze,* and *Akebono.*

Now came the Dauntless dive bombers and Avenger torpedo bombers from the other TG 38.3 units. Cmdr. Ed Craig of *USS Langley's* AG 44 went after damaged destroyer *Naganami,* leading his Avengers into the destroyer in one torpedo drop after another. Although most of the fish missed, three of them struck the destroyer squarely and opened huge holes in the hull. Uncontrolled sea water poured into the holds and the stricken Japanese destroyer went down.

Lt. Cmdr. Ed Anderson of *Ticonderoga's* AG

80 led his 12 dive bombers after the 8,000 ton freighter *Akitsushima Maru*. "We'll hit her in pairs, in pairs! Each element will remain at least 30 seconds behind the first."

"Yes sir," Lt. Charles Shuttuck answered.

The gunners aboard the freighter as well as AA gunners aboard Japanese destroyers fired desperately at the diving Dauntlessess. The Japanese shot down two of *Ticonderoga*'s planes, but they did not stop the attack. Whistling 500 pounders came down on *Akitsushima Maru*. Most of the bombs missed, but at least two struck home. The explosions wrecked the superstructure, ignited raging fires, and destroyed equipment. However, Japanese sailors, working desperately, stopped flooding and contained flames. The ship's commander refused to abandon the vessel and he urged his crew to a herculean effort to save the cargo ship.

Thus in a matter of minutes the first attacking formation from TF 38 had sunk three ships and damaged several others. Admiral Matsuyama anxiously ordered a reformation of his flotilla to continue on to Ormoc Bay. He also called Manila and frantically asked for more air support.

"The enemy will no doubt send more carrier aircraft to attack us. We must have massive air cover if we are to save the remainder of our vessels."

But the Japanese would not stop the TF 38 carrier force today as they could not stop the U.S. 5th Air Force yesterday.

At 0930 hours, the next swarm of U.S. navy

planes took off from the TG 38.1 carriers. Aboard *Hornet,* Cmdr. Fred Schraeder zoomed off the deck with 12 torpedo bombers from AG 11. Right behind him, Lt. Cmdr. Farrington roared off *Hornet* with 12 more torpedo bombers. From *USS Cowpens,* Lt. Cmdr. Tom Jenkins led 12 torpedo bombers, and from *USS Monterey,* Lt. Cmdr. Ron Gift zoomed off the deck with 12 more torpedo bombers.

12 Hellcats from *Hornet,* another dozen from *Cowpens,* and 16 Hellcats from *Monterey* also took off. These 40 fighters would escort the 52 torpedo bombers from TG 38.1.

Meanwhile, the Japanese attempted to stop the next formation of U.S. carrier planes. From his Clark Field headquarters on Luzon, Gen. Kyoji Tominga issued frantic orders: "You will mount every available fighter plane. Every plane possible! Notify Commander Nakajima of the 331st Kokutai and Captain Okamura of the 22nd Air Brigade. We must protect Admiral Matsuyama's convoy."

"Yes, Honorable Tominga."

"We must have 100 aircraft over the convoy, if necessary," Tominga raved on.

Both Tadashi Nakajima and Mutohara Okamura acted swiftly. On Luzon, Nakajima sent out 24 Zeros of the 2nd Fighter Squadron under Lt. Muto Yokoyama. On Negros Island, Captain Okamura sent off 30 Oscars under Lt. Satashi Anabuki of the 331st Sentai and 36 Jacks under Lt. Yonosoki Iguchi of the 352nd Sentai. However, these 90 4th Base Air Force planes would not arrive over the lower Sibuyan Sea before the next American carrier plane attack.

At 1030 hours, Cmdr. Frank Schraeder of *USS Hornet* reached the reforming Convoy Three with his 24 torpedo bombers. He cried into his TBS. "Okay, in pairs; single out your target and go after it."

"Yes sir," Lt. Cmdr. Bob Farrington said.

Schraeder led the first element of four Avengers against destroyer *Shimakaze* that had been damaged earlier by *Essex* planes. Heavy AA fire from the zigzagging destroyer pelted the oncoming American torpedo bombers. Two flak hits shattered one Avenger and the torpedo bomber cartwheeled into the sea, killing the crew. However, the other Avengers came within 500 yards of *Shimakaze* before Schraeder and his companions dropped their 1,000 pound torpedoes. One fish missed but the other two hit squarely in the starboard midsection and starboard forward. Two numbing explosions shuddered the 2100 ton warship, with one blast igniting the destroyer's magazine.

Schraeder turned for a look and saw the stricken destroyer going down in a hiss of steam. Dozens of Japanese sailors and their soldier passengers, *Shimakaze's* survivors, were soon floundering in the sea.

The other Avengers pilots in Schraeder's squadron dropped more torpedoes among the other convoy vessels. One torpedo damaged transport *Koa Maru* and others damaged destroyer *Akishimo*. A third struck *Koshii 22* for the second torpedo hit on the small vessel this morning. Still, the pesky coastal defense vessel remained afloat and churned under her own power.

Lt. Cmdr. Bob Farrington, meanwhile, took his four plane element and skimmed toward a fat transport, *Kobyo Maru,* a 10,000 tonner that carried some 2,000 26th Division troops, along with 500 tons of supplies and arms. Convoy Three destroyers fired AA guns at the four zooming Avengers, since the Japanese wanted desperately to save this maru. The heavy flak knocked down two of the U.S. torpedo bombers and Farrington's wingman cried into his TBS.

"Commander, the flak's too heavy; maybe we better back off."

"Like hell," Farrington answered. "We're too goddamn close to that fat cat to give up now."

Miraculously, none of the heavy anti-aircraft bursts hit the two Avengers, and Farrington and his wingman came within an astonishing 300 yards before dropping their torpedoes. Both fish ran straight and true, slamming into the port midsection of *Kobyo Maru.* A pair of concussioning explosions followed and the blasts opened the entire port side. Tons of sea water poured into the ship like a deluge from a broken dam. The big transport listed quickly to starboard and within minutes she capsized and went down.

The quick loss of the big transport horrified Japanese sailors and soldiers in Convoy Three. The ship had sunk so swiftly that less than 100 soldiers of the 2,000 man complement and less than ten sailors of the 100 man crew survived the

Kobyo Maru sinking.

Now came the torpedo bombers from *Cowpens* and *Monterey*. Lt. Cmdr. Tom Jenkins led an element of four torpedo bombers toward the damaged transport *Koa Maru* that had slowed to a crawl from an earlier hit by a *Hornet* Avenger. The gunners aboard the transport tried to ward off the oncoming torpedo bombers. But to no avail. Jenkins and three fellow pilots skimmed over the water and, despite flak hits, they sent four torpedoes streaking toward the big transport. Three missed, but the fourth struck the port aft and shuddered the maru to a stop. The ship quickly listed to ten degrees.

Japanese sailors aboard the ship worked furiously to stop flooding, but the efforts would prove futile. Other *Cowpens* torpedo bombers also streaked after the transport and unleashed more fish that streaked towards the vessel. Three more torpedoes hit the big transport and opened the entire port side. The ship was finished, and its commander ordered abandon ship. However, more than 500 26th Division troops and 500 tons of supplies went down with *Koa Maru*.

Now came the Avengers from *Monterey*'s AG 28. Lt. Cmdr. Ron Gift focused his attention on zigzagging destroyer *Hamani,* the flagship of Convoy Three. He picked up his TBS. "Our first element is going after that destroyer. First two aircraft will hit on the forward and second two aircraft will strike on the aft."

"Okay, Ron," Lt. Tom Driess answered.

Both Gift and Driess had been in combat over a

year and they had already sunk three Japanese ships between them. They had also damaged several more ships in various sea battles, including the renowned Battle of the Philippine Sea. Now, they sought the fourth surface ship kill of their combat careers.

Aboard *Hamani,* Admiral Matsuyama stared in terror at the four oncoming Avengers and he cried frantically into his radio phone. "You must destroy them; you must! Helmsman, turn quickly to starboard!"

But, neither Matsuyama's AA gunners nor his pilot house crew could stem the Avenger attack. Gift and his wingman came into the ship on the forward and released two torpedoes that hit and exploded, blowing off the entire prow, before tons of water poured into the destroyer. Seconds later, Tom Driess and his wingman sent a pair of torpedoes into the aft quarter of *Hamani.* More numbing explosions rocked the 2,200 ton destroyer. As the ship listed quickly and started down, Matsuyama yelled into his radio.

"Damage! Report damage!"

"There is no hope, Honorable Matsuyama," the damage control officer said. "We must abandon ship at once or we are all lost."

"Very well," the Convoy Three commander answered in resignation.

Sixty-seven of *Hamani*'s 210 man crew went down with the destroyer. However, Matsuyama jumped safely into the sea and he would be among the survivors who were later fished out of the water.

By the time the planes from TG 38.3 and TG 38.1 had left the Sibuyan Sea, seven ships from Convoy Three were already down or going down. Most of the rest were damaged.

Adm. Akira Shoji, from his headquarters in Manila, listened in disbelief to the vast destruction against his convoy, including the loss of flag destroyer *Hamani*. He also worried about Admiral Matsuyama, the flotilla commander. He did not know if his good friend and courageous flag leader had survived or if he had gone down in the Sibuyan Sea. He made a frantic call to General Tominga at Clark Field.

"I do not know how many vessels are still afloat, but they must have protection, they must."

"The squadrons of fighters are on the way," Tominga said. "I can assure you there will be no more losses."

"I hope not," Shoji said.

And, in fact, 90 Japanese fighter planes were now reaching the crippled Convoy Three. A PBY sighted the huge 4th Base Air Force air armada and the American observer quickly called TF 58. The report disturbed Admiral Sherman, who did not have enough ammo and fuel to send out a large cover of fighters for his next formation of Bombers, Dauntlesses and Avengers from TG 38.4 that were preparing to take off. However, he suddenly remembered the promise from Gen. Ennis Whitehead. "Call 5th Air Force in Leyte. Tell them we need fighter cover for the next carrier strike on that convoy."

"Yes sir."

When the request reached Tacloban, Gen. Ennis Whitehead never hesitated. He ordered off fighters from all five squadrons based in Leyte. They would rendezvous with the carrier bombers over San Bernadino Strait and escort them to the Sibuyan Sea. Col. Charles MacDonald quickly took off with 32 P-38s from his 475th Group's 432nd and 431st Squadrons, while Lt. Col. Bob Morrissey took off with 32 P-38s from the 49th Group's 9th and 7th Squadrons. Capt. Rube Archuleta took off with 12 P-40s from the 110th Recon Squadron, leaving only the P-61s behind to guard Tacloban. The 76 U.S. Army Air Force planes would engage the Japanese fighter planes, so the TG 38.4 navy bombers could hit Convoy Three still again.

"Keep the formations tight, keep them tight," Morrissey told his pilots. "They say the Nips have about a hundred planes hanging over that convoy."

"Goddamn, Bobby," Maj. Dick Bong answered Morrissey over the radio, "we're in for another good donnybrook. I can't wait."

And indeed, the next air battle between American and Japanese fighter pilots would be the biggest yet in the brawling air-sea fights that had raged for two days in the central Philippines.

Chapter Fourteen

Cmdr. Arisho Kamiro, skipper of destroyer *Akebono,* was now technically in command of Convoy Three since Admiral Matsuyama and his flotilla staff were missing. After the loss of flag destroyer *Hamani,* no one knew how many of the flag officers, if any, had survived the sinking. So, the Convoy Three command fell to Kamiro, a veteran of several naval battles in the Pacific, including the sea fights in the Solomons, the Marshalls, and the more recent battles of Leyte.

The *Akebono* skipper contacted every convoy ship he could to evaluate damage and losses, and the reports shocked him. Kamiro learned that three transport marus had gone down along with oiler *Jinei Maru,* while freighter *Akitsushima Maru* was badly damaged. Most of the 26th Division troops and tons of supplies had been lost. Further, three destroyers were down or going down. Convoy Three had been left with only two coastal defense ships, four destroyers and the damaged freighter.

Kamiro saw no point in continuing the sail to

Ormoc Bay since he had only 800 of the 26th Division troops accounted for, soldiers aboard the destroyer-transports *Maki* and *Wakatsuki*. He decided to rescue as many men as possible from the sea and then head back to Manila Bay.

"All ships will cover as much area as possible," the commander told Lt. Taro Saro, the *Akebono* executive officer. "We will spend as much time as necessary to rescue whatever soldiers and sailors we can. We will then set a course for a return to Luzon."

"Yes, Honorable Commander," Saro said.

Kamiro was not too concerned about further air attacks since 90 fighter planes from the 4th Base Air Force now loitered over the battered Convoy Three: 24 Zeros of the 2nd Squadron under Lieutenant Yokoyama, 30 Oscars of the 351st Sentai under Lieutenant Anabuki, and 26 Jacks of the 352nd Sentai under Lieutenant Iguchi. This mass of planes would surely thwart any new U.S. air formation that attempted more attacks on the convoy. Kamiro looked at Lieutenant Saro.

"You will tell all ship commanders to work with all haste. Many of our soldiers and sailors may drown if we do not rescue them swiftly."

"Yes, Commander."

Arisho Kamiro watched the rescue operations calmly and confidently. However, at 1130 hours, he heard the drone of planes to the southeast. Whoop alarms again echoed from the surviving ships of Convoy Three as enemy planes approached the area. These new visitors were the 76 U.S. fighter planes out of Tacloban.

Colonel MacDonald saw the Japanese fighter planes ahead and he cried into his radio. "There's that army of Nip fighters—right up ahead."

"Goddamn," Bong cried, "I never saw so many Nips in one place before."

"All units, climb high," MacDonald cried into his radio again. "Stick to your wingmen. You're going to need him with that swarm of bandits. We've got to scatter those enemy planes in a hurry because the navy bombers are right behind us."

"We read you, Colonel," Maj. Tom McGuire said.

Meanwhile, Lt. Moto Yokoyama of the Japanese 2nd Squadron saw the oncoming American planes, and he too cried into his radio. "Our squadron will fly high and attack the first formations of enemy planes. 351st Sentai will attack the rear element of American aircraft, and the 352nd Sentai will supply reinforcement aircraft as necessary."

"We will do so," Lieutenant Anabuki said.

"My sentai will remain high until called on," Lieutenant Iguchi said.

On the surface of the sea, the sailors aboard the Japanese ships constantly shuttled their glances between the floundering men in the water who awaited rescue and the countless planes overhead that darted about the sky. They listened and watched as screaming planes arced and dived, while chattering machine gun fire and hissing cannon shells echoed across the sky.

Above the sea, Col. Charles MacDonald and his wing man claimed two Zeros with quick machine gun bursts. One plane exploded in midair while the other flamed in a big arc and then splashed into the sea. From the same 432nd Squadron Maj. John Loisel and his wingman jumped a trio of Oscars, blowing one Japanese plane apart and chopping the wing off the second plane. They ripped the tail off the third Oscar. All three victims plunged into the sea.

In the 475th Fighter Group's 431st Squadron, Maj. Tom McGuire, with Capt. Joe Moreing and Capt. Bob Cline, downed an incredible seven planes in less than a minute, during two murderous passes. McGuire raised his score to 34 kills when he shattered one Oscar with thumping 37mm shells, smashed the cockpit and killed the pilot of a second plane, and split the fuselage of the third enemy aircraft with heavy wing fire. All three 351st Sentai planes dropped into the sea. Captain Moreing got two Oscars, knocking one out of the air with .50 caliber bursts that clipped off the wing, and downing the other plane with 37mm hits that destroyed the cockpit and killed the pilot. Bob Cline got his two kills with chattering machine gun fire from three o'clock high. He riddled the fuselage of one plane that flipped over and fluttered into the sea. He downed the second Oscar with telling tracer hits that ignited the gas tank.

90 Japanese planes were not enough for 76 superior U.S. fighter planes and their superior pilots. So, the slaughter continued.

49th Fighter Group airmen also scored heavily. From the 9th Squadron, Lt. Col. Bob Morrissey got two Zeros of Yokoyama's 2nd Squadron when he caught a trio of Japanese planes off guard. Morrissey's machine bursts hit the fuel tank of one Zero that exploded. The lieutenant colonel knocked the nose off of the second victim with 37mm shellfire. From the same squadron, Lt. Bill Huiseman tailed an unsuspecting Zero pilot and riddled his plane with bursts of machine gun fire. Capt. Bill Williams came down on a surprised Japanese pilot and blew off the plane's tail with exploding 37mm shells.

The new Jack fighters were no better than the Oscar and Zeros against the adept, aggressive American pilots. Maj. Jerry Johnson and his wingman of the 7th Squadron chased a trio of Jacks, opening with chattering .50 caliber fire from 600 yards. The heavy tracer fire from the two U.S. pilots downed a pair of the planes and damaged the third. Capt. Bob DeHaven and his wingman also bounced a trio of Jacks, spraying the three aircraft with telling .50 caliber fire. All three Japanese planes burst into flames from the heavy barrage before the enemy aircraft flamed into the sea.

Amidst the countless targets, the incomparable Dick Bong downed three planes to maintain his score lead over the equally adept Tom McGuire. In two passes, Bong sent three Jacks into the sea to raise his score to 38 victories. The major downed the first with a savage 37mm shell hit on the nose that blew away the Jack's engine. He got the second score when he sliced off the wing of an enemy plane with chattering machine gun fire, and

Bong got his third when another thumping 37mm cannon hit exploded in the fuselage and cut the Japanese plane in half.

Even the P-40 airmen of the 110th Recon Squadron did well, especially at the lower altitudes. The Warhawk pilots downed seven Zeros. Capt. Rube Archuleta, Lt. Bob Turner, and Lt. Roy Rube destroyed two Japanese planes each.

Within a half hour, the Americans from Tacloban had downed 43 Japanese fighter planes for a loss of two P-38s and one P-40, an astounding rout. Lieutenant Yokoyama, Lieutenant Anabuki, and Lieutenant Iguchi then spent most of their efforts trying to regroup the panicked, stampeding survivors of their squadrons. Before they could do so, however, the action in the Sibuyan Sea would be over. No sooner had the dogfights broken off, when the next swarm of U.S. Navy TF 38 bombers roared over the Sibuyan Sea—nearly 60 dive bombers and torpedo bombers from TG 38.4's *USS Franklin, Enterprise, San Jacinto,* and *Belleau Woods.*

Cmdr. Arishio Kamiro frowned in frustration. He could do nothing but suspend rescue operations and revert to protective measures. "All gunners will man weapons; man weapons at once! Helmsmen, resume evasive courses."

"Yes, Commander," Lt. Taro Saro said.

Miraculously for the Japanese, this last formation of TF 38 planes did not do as much damage as had the first two formations of U.S. Navy bombers. The American airmen were now attacking speedy warships, small destroyers and small coastal defense ships that could more easily avoid gliding bombs or skimming torpedoes, and that could send up heavy AA fire.

Still, Lt. Cmdr. Bob French led 12 torpedo bombers of *Franklin's* AG 13 toward a pair of destroyers, damaged *Wakatsuki* and zigzagging *Maki,* two warships that carried 26th Division soldiers. French roared toward *Wakatsuki* with six planes. In pairs, the sextet of Avengers dropped a half dozen torpedoes. Four missed, but two slammed into the starboard forward and exploded, blowing a pair of 12 foot holes out of the hull. Tons of water poured into the destroyer that settled by the bow. Most of the sailors and soldier passengers went down with her.

"We got her, Commander, we got her," Lieutenant Skinner cried.

"She's going down, no doubt about that," French answered.

Other planes from TG 38.4 attacked the remnants of Convoy Three, but most of the bombs and torpedoes missed as Japanese helmsmen deftly zigged and zagged away from the Dauntlesses and Avengers. However, a 500 pounder struck coastal defense ship *Koshii 22* to further damage this ship. Another bomb ignited more fires on destroyer *Akebono* and Commander Kamiro screamed quick orders to douse the flames. Still another bomb hit the already damaged destroyer *Maki* to wreck more of the warship's superstructure.

Finally, two torpedoes from carrier *San Jacinto*

aircraft slammed into the damaged freighter *Akitsushima Maru*. The big cargo ship, already badly damaged, could not maneuver like the small warships. The two hits shuddered the 10,000 ton vessel in its final death throes and the ship went down in the Sibuyan Sea, taking more than 5,000 tons of supplies with her.

When these fast U.S. carrier planes left the Sibuyan Sea, only the coastal defense vessel *Koshii 29* remained unscathed. Four destroyers were down, all five marus were down, while destroyers *Maki, Akebono* and *Arishimo* had been quite badly damaged. The defense vessel *Koshii 22* was burning and listing and would be abandoned by the end of the day.

The Japanese had lost more than 6,000 tons of the 6,600 tons of supplies that Convoy Three had carried. Further, less then 2,000 soldiers of the 12,000 man 26th Division had been rescued from the sea. Finally, the Japanese fighter squadrons had lost nearly 100 more Oscars, Zeros, and Jacks to the TG 38 and 5th Air Force fighter planes in the Japanese vain attempts to stop the three U.S. carrier strikes on Admiral Matsuyama's flotilla.

The Japanese had sent out 36 ships from Manila Bay and Cagayan to reinforce Leyte with men and supplies. Only the men of the 1st Division had reached Leyte, while the handful of rescued 26th and 30th Division survivors had been carried back to Luzon or Mindanao. All of the more than 10,000 tons of supplies, arms, and ammunition in the three convoys had gone to the bottom of the sea. The 4th Base Air Force had lost more than

300 of its fighters and bombers in the futile attempt to stop the Americans over the convoys or to knock out Tacloban.

The 5th Air Force airmen from the 18th, 49th, 348th, and 475th Fighter Groups, along with airmen of the 110th Recon Squadron, had done a remarkable job in stopping Japanese air power. The 38th Bomb Group skip bombers had utterly devastated two of the reinforcement convoys, while the airmen of the U.S. Navy's TG 31.1, TG 38.1, and TG 38.4 had done an equally successful job in almost wiping out Convoy Three.

For the Americans, the 48 hour period from late 9 November to late 11 November 1944 had ended in brilliant victory. They had lost 26 aircraft in their multiple dogfights with planes from the Japanese 4th Base Air Force or from 1st Transportation Fleet AA fire.

Thanks to American airmen, the TA Operation had ended in dismal failure.

Yet, neither General Yamashita, commander of all forces in the Philippines, nor General Suzuki, commander of the 35th Army in Leyte, was willing to give up. They insisted that both Admiral Shoji of the 1st Transportation Fleet and General Tominga of the 4th Base Air Force continue to carry and protect reinforcements to Leyte. However, Shoji had few marus left to carry men and supplies, and even fewer warships to escort such merchant ships. Tominga learned from Commander Nakajima of the 331st Kokutai and Captain Okamura of the 22nd Air Brigade that

neither wing had more than a few planes left to escort ships on the high seas or to conduct bombing missions against Tacloban.

The last and most intense dogfight on 11 November had all but finished the 4th Base Air Force fighter units. The Americans now dominated completely the skies over the Central Philippines.

Tominga reluctantly called on Adm. Tajijiro Onishi to use Kamikaze planes in new efforts to protect ships on the way to Leyte. But the suicide pilots failed even more miserably against aggressive American fighter pilots and fighter-bombers. Few ships reached Leyte during the remainder of November.

In the ground war, Gen. Tadasu Kotaoka led his Gem Division troops into battle with a minimum of food, supplies, ammunition and arms. He and his soldiers fought hard, but the 1st Division, that proud unit from Manchuria, slowly collapsed before the growing American ground strength. By the end of November, American GIs had pushed Japanese troops out of central Leyte. The fresh U.S. 1st Cavalry, 24th Infantry, and 32nd Infantry Division forced Japanese units into a defensive pocket in and around the town of Ormoc.

Then, at dawn of 7 December 1944, on the third anniversary of Pearl Harbor, the 77th and 96th U.S. Infantry Divisions landed on the shores of Ormoc Bay just below the town of Ormoc. By 0930 hours, all troops had gone ashore, some 30,000 GIs. Overhead, hundreds of planes from the U.S. Navy's TF 38 carrier force and the U.S. Army's 5th Air Force darkened the sky. Only a few formations of suicide planes challenged the huge amphibious armada. The Kamikazes did sink destroyers USS Ward and USS Mahan, but at the cost of more than a 100 Kamikazes.

Even as the Americans tightened the trap against the Japanese 35th Army on Leyte, more U.S. troops landed on Mindoro Island to cut off once and for all the supply route between Luzon and the beleaguered troops on Leyte. By the first of the year, the battle for Leyte was over.

The Japanese had lost 80,557 killed in the vicious battle for Leyte, with 828 prisoners. Thirteen thousand Japanese troops, including Gen. Sosaku Suzuki, CinC of the 35th Army, Gen. Tadasu Kotaoka, commander of the 1st Division, and Lt. Minetoshi Yahiro, the company commander, escaped the last ditch Japanese stand at Ormoc. Yahiro's battalion commander, Maj. Itusi Imada, and the lieutenant's chief NCO, Sgt. Kiyoshi Kamiko, were killed in the fighting. General Suzuki, after surviving the Leyte fight, was killed in an American bombing raid on Negros Island in April of 1945.

No one knows how many Japanese sailors and airmen perished during the Leyte campaign. However, from U.S. Strategic Bombing Survey interviews after the war, U.S. evaluators concluded that the Japanese had lost at least 25,000 sailors and 5,000 airmen in the fight for Leyte.

However, the Americans had not escaped lightly. The U.S. 6th Army, including the 5th Air Force, had suffered 15,584 battle casualties, including 3,508 killed. The U.S. Navy, including carrier airmen, had suffered 21,000 battle casualties, with 1,615 killed or missing in action. Yet, the conquest of Leyte had opened the way for the next leap toward Japan's homeland.

More than anything else, the twin air punches of the U.S. Army 5th Air Force and the U.S. Navy's TF 38 had been the most successful of the Pacific war. The combined army-navy aerial assaults of 9-11 November had been the most decisive aspect of the Leyte campaign, for these attacks broke the back of the Japanese 35th Army defense plans. Adm. Muto Matsuyama told American interrogators after the war:

"The highly successful air attacks on the three convoys of the TA Operation ended all hope of saving Leyte. The massive losses inflicted by the American air units not only deprived General Suzuki of reinforcements in men and supplies, but also decimated the 1st Transportation Fleet and the 4th Base Air Force. We no longer had ships and aircraft to successfully hold Leyte. By the first of the year, 1945, General Yamashita and everyone else in the 14th Army Group staff realized that we would need to abandon all of the Philippines except Luzon and make our final stand here."

In Manila, Gen. Tomoyuki Yamashita himself offered discouraging words to his staff after the TA Operation fiasco. "We have lost the decisive battle. It is impossible for a second chance. We can do nothing more than strengthen our position on Luzon and even such defenses may not stop the enemy. Let us pray to the spirits of our heavenly ancestors and hope they answer our supplications to hold Luzon as they failed to answer our supplications for holding Leyte."

For the airmen of the 5th Air Force, the 38th Bomb Group Sunsetters won a DUC for its "Exceptional devotion to duty when, in the face of intense anti-aircraft fire, the group inflicted severe losses on the enemy armada and crushed the Japanese attempt to send in more troops against our ground forces at Leyte."

The 18th Fighter Group's 70th Squadron won a DUC for "Braving intense anti-aircraft fire and enemy interceptors to conduct a vigorous attack on a Japanese convoy attempting to bring reinforcements to Leyte."

The 49th Fighter Group won a DUC for its "Intense operations against the Japanese at Leyte on 9-11 November, with Major Richard Bong winning the CMH for "The destruction of eight enemy aircraft over Ormoc Bay during a 48 hour period."

The 475th Fighter Group won a DUC for "Destroying hordes of Japanese planes in the air while escorting American bombers in attacks on Japanese ships in Ormoc Bay." The 110th Tactical Recon Squadron also won a DUC for "Courageously attacking both Japanese ships and enemy aircraft in the successful Ormoc Bay air campaign."

The U.S. Navy also won high praises and commendations. All three carrier groups of TF 38 won DUC's for their "Exceptional attacks on a Japanese reinforcement convoy in the Sibuyan Sea on 11 November 1944, in which the air units totally destroyed the enemy convoy."

When the Leyte campaign ended, General Walter Krueger praised both the 5th Air Force and TF 38. "We could have never taken Leyte without the excellent air support from American army and navy air units. They turned Ormoc Bay into a graveyard for Japanese ships. The enemy has always boasted about the bravery of their troops, but they'll never match the courage and determination of our own airmen, soldiers, and sailors."

PARTICIPANTS

AMERICAN

6th Army
  CinC—General Walter Krueger
  Chief of Staff—General Steven Chamberlain
  34th Infantry Regiment—Colonel Thomas Clifford
  Also: 24th Division, 7th Division, 96th Division
5th Air Force
  CinC—General Ennis Whitehead
  28th Air Depot—Colonel Lief Sverdrup
  308th Bomb Wing—Colonel Dan Hutchinson
  38th Bomb Group—Colonel Edward Gavin
    822nd Squadron—Major Edward McClean
    405th Squadron—Major Edward Maurer
    71st Squadron—Lt. Col. Edward Hawes
    823rd Squadron—Captain John Irick
  49th Fighter Group—Colonel George Walker
    7th Squadron—Major Jerry Johnson
    9th Squadron—Lt. Col. Bob Morrissey
  475th Fighter Group—Colonel Charles MacDonald
    431st Squadron—Major Tom McGuire
    432nd Squadron—Major John Loisel
  460th Fighter Squadron, 348th Group—Major William Dunham
  110th Tactical Recon Squadron—Captain Rubel Archuleta
  70th Fighter Squadron, 18th Group—Major William Cowper
5th U.S. Fleet—Admiral Thomas Kinkaid
  TF 38—Admiral Fred Sherman
    TG 38.3, AG 4, *USS Essex*—Cmdr. James Mini
      Also AG 44—*Langley*, AG 80—*Ticonderoga*
    TG 38.1, AG 11, *USS Hornet,* Cmdr. Frank Schraeder
      Also AG 22—*Cowpens*, AG 28—*Monterey*
    TG 38.4, AG 13, *USS Franklin,* Cmdr. Robert French
      Also, AG 20—*Enterprise*, AG 51—*San Jacinto*, AG 21—*Belleau Woods*
  7th Amphibious Fleet—Admiral Daniel Darbey

JAPANESE

14th Area Army

   CinC—General Tomoyuki Yamashita

   Chief of Staff—General Toshi Mishimura

   35th Army—General Sosoku Suzuki

     102nd Division—General Shimpei Fukue

     26th Division—General Susumo Makino

     1st Division—General Tadasu Kotaoka

     46th Regiment—Colonel Mitsui Yosuka

     Also: 16 Division, 68th Brigade, 20 Regiment

4th Base Air Force

   CinC—General Kyoji Tominga

     331st Kokutai (Navy)—Cmdr. Tadashi Nakajima

       1st Squadron—Lt. Makase Ibusuki

       2nd Squadron—Lt. Muto Yokoyama

       3rd Squadron—Lt. Cmdr. Chiuchi Yoshiota

     22nd Air Brigade (Army)—Captain Mutohara Okamura

       351st Sentai—Lt. Satashi Anabuki

       352nd Sentai—Lt. Yonosoki Iguchi

       351st Sentai—Lt. Ota Tsubo

     201st Air Group (Kamikaze)—Admiral Takijiro Onishi

Southeast Area Fleet—Admiral Denshichi Okochi

   1st Transportation Fleet—Admiral Akira Shoji, CinC

                  Admiral Sato Tomioka, Chief of Staff

   Convoy One—Admiral Matsuji Ijuin

   Convoy Two—Cmdr. Noriteru Yatsui

   Convoy Three—Admiral Muto Matsuyama

BIBLIOGRAPHY

Books:

Birdsall, Steven, *Flying Buccaneers,* Doubleday & Co., Garden City, NY, 1977

Cannon, M. Hamlin, *Leyte: Return to the Philippines,* OCMH, Department of the Army, Washington, DC, 1954

Constable, Trevor; Toliver, Raymond, *Fighter Aces of the U.S.A.,* Aero Publishers, Fallbrook, Calif., 1979

Craven, Wesley, Cates, James, *U.S. Army Air Force in World War II, Volume V, The Pacific: Matterhorn to Nagasaki,* Univ. of Chicago Press, Chicago, 1953

Dull, Paul, *The Imperial Japanese Navy,* Naval Institute Press, Annapolis, 1978

Fitzsimmons, Bernard, *War Planes and Air Battles of World War II,* Beckman House Publishers, New York, 1973

Haugland, Vernon, *AAF Against Japan,* Harper Bros., New York, 1948

Henry, John, *History of the 38th Bomb Group,* Aerospace Publishers, Kansas State Univ. Press, Manhattan, Kansas, 1978

Hess, William N., *Pacific Sweep,* Doubleday & Co., New York, 1974

Jablonski, Edward, *Air War: Wings of Fire,* Doubleday & Co., Garden City, NY, 1971

Jackson, Robert, *Fighter Pilots of World War II,* St. Martin Press, New York, 1976

Karig, Walter; Harris, Russell; Manson, Frank, *Battle Report: Victory in the Pacific,* Rinehart & Company, New York, 1949

Morrison, Samuel, *U.S. Navy in World War II: Volume XII, Leyte,* Little, Brown Company, Boston, 1963

Millot, Bernard, *Divine Thunder,* McCall Publishers, New York, 1970

Pineau, Roger; Saito, Fred, *Japanese Destroyer Captain,* Ballantine Books, New York, 1961

Potter, John Dean, *The Life and Death of a Japanese General,* Frederick Muller Ltd., London, Eng., 1962

Rust, Kenneth, *5th Air Force Story,* Historical Aviation

Album, Temple City, Calif., 1973

Sims, Edward, *American Aces,* Harper & Bros., New York, 1958

Toland, John, *The Rising Sun,* Random House, New York, 1970

Archive Sources:

Historical Research Center, Maxwell Air Force Base, Montgomery, Ala.

 5th Air Force—Weekly Intelligence Summaries, 11/5/44—11/12/44

 5th Air Force—Weekly Review #50A-2, 11/5/44—11/12/44

 38th Bomb Group Combat Action Report, 11/10/44

 38th Bomb Group Final Mission Report, FO 315-2-A1, 11/10/44

  71st Bomb Squadron Narrative Report (Ormoc Bay) 11/11/44

  822nd Bomb Squadron Narrative Report (Ormoc Bay) 11/11/44

  823rd Bomb Squadron Narrative Report (Ormoc Bay) 11/11/44

  405th Bomb Squadron Narrative Report (Ormoc Bay) 11/11/44

 49th Fighter Group, Monthly Summary of Action Reports, 11/1/44—11/30/44

 70th Fighter Squadron Monthly Summary of Action Reports, 11/1/44—11/30/44

 345th Bomb Group, Combat Action Report, 11/9/44

 348th Fighter Group, Monthly Summary of Action Reports, 11/1/44—11/30/44

 475th Fighter Group, Monthly Summary of Action Reports, 11/1/44—11/30/44

USS Strategic Bombing Survey, Interrogation of Japanese Officers

  #159, Cmdr. Noriteru Yatsui, ''Reinforcement & Support of Leyte Campaign''

  #229, Admiral Muto Matsuyama, ''Escort Duty in

the Philippines"

#355, Admiral S. Tomioka, "Japanese Naval Actions, 1944"

#354, Col. Junji Hayashi, "Japanese Army Air Force in the Philippines"

#454, Admiral Akira Shoji, "Operations of 1st Transportation Fleet in the Philippines"

#16946, General Yoshiharu Tomochika, "True Facts: Report of Leyte Operations"

U.S. Navy Historical Center, Washington Navy Yard Washington DC

Cincpac Monthly Reports, Series #00204, November 1944

MacArthur Historical Report #387

Cincpac Weekly Intelligence Summary #4

TF 38 War Diary for Oct.—Nov. 1944

USS Essex Action Reports, November 1944

USS Monterey Action Reports, November 1944

USS Ticonderoga Action Reports, November 1944

USS Franklin Action Reports, November 1944

USS Hornet Action Reports, November 1944

Halsey 5th Fleet Historical Report, period 27 Oct.—30 Nov. 1944

Murray, Adm. George, "Carrier Support of Leyte Campaign"

Interviews of former pilots on Ormoc Bay mission at 38th Bomb Group Association

John Bellanger   Zane Corbin
Robert Blair   Edward Gavin
Harry Bradley   John Irick

Newspaper articles: New York Times

Nov. 11, 1944, "Bong Downs 34th Plane in Japanese Convoy Fight"

Nov. 11, 1944, "Rip Up Big Japanese Troop Convoy"

Nov. 12, 1944, "Fight in Ormoc Bay Costs Foe Heavily"

Aerospace Historian Magazine
    Clark, Dean, "A B-25 Over Ormoc"
    Henry, John, "The Battle of Ormoc Bay"

MAPS: All maps from National Archives and U.S. Navy Historical Center

PHOTOS:
    DAVA Still Picture Branch (including Izawa collection of Japanese)
    National Archives, Washington, DC
    U.S. Navy Department, Washington, DC
    Ret. Col. Edward Gavin, Ret. Gen. Lawrence Tanberg, Ret. Captain Zane Corbin

Note: The author would like to thank Mr. Ken Darrow, Portland, Oregon, Mr. Edward Gavin, Sante Fe, NM, and Mr. John Irick, Albuquerque, NM, for their excellent help in obtaining detailed information on the 38th Bomb Group's participation in the attack on the Japanese resupply convoys at Ormoc Bay, 10 November 1944.

MORE EXCITING READING!

VALOR AT LEYTE (1213, $3.25)
by Lawrence Cortesi
Leyte, The Philippines. The Japanese were entrenched and willing to sacrifice everything to hold the island. And as troop ships carrying reinforcements for the Emperor's line steamed into Ormoc Bay, the valiant American fliers came in on one of the most important missions of the war!

IWO (799, $2.75)
by Richard Wheeler
For five weeks in 1945, Iwo Jima saw some of the most intense combat in history. This is the story of that devastating battle, told from the perspective of both the U.S. Marines who invaded the island and the Japanese soldiers who defended it.

VICTORY AT GUADALCANAL (1198, $3.50)
by Robert Edward Lee
For six months and two days, combined U.S. Army and Marine forces held off the Japanese assault on Guadalcanal. It was the longest single battle in the history of American warfare—and marked the end of Japanese advances in the Pacific!

PACIFIC HELLFIRE (1179, $3.25)
by Lawrence Cortesi
The Japanese were entrenched at Truk. We had to take it before we could move into the Marianas. And before the battle was over, many valiant American sailors and airmen sacrificed their lives. But sixteen Japanese ships went to the bottom—shortening the war by at least a year!

Available wherever paperbacks are sold, or order direct from the Publisher. Send cover price plus 50¢ per copy for mailing and handling to Zebra Books, 475 Park Avenue South, New York, N.Y. 10016. DO NOT SEND CASH.

THE SURVIVALIST SERIES
by Jerry Ahern

#1: TOTAL WAR (960, $2.50)

The first in the shocking series that follows the unrelenting search for ex-CIA covert operations officer John Thomas Rourke to locate his missing family—after the button is pressed, the missiles launched and the multimegaton bombs unleashed . . .

#2: THE NIGHTMARE BEGINS (810, $2.50)

After WW III, the United States is just a memory. But ex-CIA covert operations officer Rourke hasn't forgotten his family. While hiding from the Soviet occupation forces, he adheres to his search!

#3: THE QUEST (851, $2.50)

Not even a deadly game of intrigue within the Soviet High Command, the formation of the American "resistance" and a highly placed traitor in the new U.S. government can deter Rourke from continuing his desperate search for his family.

#4: THE DOOMSAYER (893, $2.50)

The most massive earthquake in history is only hours away, and Communist-Cuban troops, Soviet-Cuban rivalry, and a traitor in the inner circle of U.S. II block Rourke's path. But he must go on—he is THE SURVIVALIST.

#5: THE WEB (1145, $2.50)

Blizzards rage around Rourke as he picks up the trail of his family and is forced to take shelter in a strangely quiet Tennessee valley town. Things seem too normal here, as if no one has heard of the War; but the quiet isn't going to last for long!

Available wherever paperbacks are sold, or order direct from the Publisher. Send cover price plus 50¢ per copy for mailing and handling to Zebra Books, 475 Park Avenue South, New York, N.Y. 10016 DO NOT SEND CASH.